Summer Weekend Cookbook

COTTAGE LIFE'S
SUMMER WEEKEND
Cookbook

RECIPES, TIPS, AND ENTERTAINING IDEAS

BY JANE RODMELL

Cataloguing in Publication Data

Rodmell, Jane, 1938 –
     Cottage life's summer weekend cookbook : recipes, tips, and entertaining ideas

Includes index.

ISBN 0-9696922-2-6

1. Cookery. I. Title. II. Title: Summer weekend cookbook.

TX829.R62 1997   641.5'64   C96-932535-5

Published by
Cottage Life Books
111 Queen St. E.
Ste. 408
Toronto, Ontario, Canada
M5C 1S2

Published in the United States by
Cottage Life Books
Box 1338
Ellicott Station
Buffalo, N.Y., U.S.A.
14205

Edited by Ann Vanderhoof
Design by Steve Manley, Overleaf Design Ltd.

Film by Fieldstone Graphics Inc.

Printed and bound in Canada by
D.W. Friesen & Sons Ltd., Altona, Manitoba

Trade distribution by
Firefly Books Ltd.
3680 Victoria Park Avenue
Willowdale, Ontario, Canada
M2H 3K1

and

Firefly Books (U.S.)
Box 1338
Ellicott Station
Buffalo, N.Y., U.S.A.
14205

To Ken, James, Patrick, and Christina

All recipes by Jane Rodmell, except as noted below:

Smoked Salmon Spirals, p. 29: Bonnie Stern
Chewy Butterscotch Bars, p. 216: Jill Snider
Chocolate Chip Crisps, p. 195: Jill Snider

Easy Apple Cake, p. 202: Jill Snider
Mix-in-the-Pan Cake, p. 206: Jill Snider
Raisin Soda Bread, p. 203: Jill Snider

The following recipes were winners in *Cottage Life* magazine's annual recipe contest:

Barbecued Marinated Brie, p. 26: Tina Roberts
Barbecued Peaches, p. 196: Nancy Weese
Caramel-Pecan Sticky Buns, p. 210: Lydia
    McClure
Chile & Cheese Squares, p. 30: Janet Donnelly
Crab Burrito Slices, p. 35: Barbara Black
Double-Chocolate Peanut Bars, p. 193: Karen
    Dolan
Double-Crust Mixed-Fruit Pie, p. 213: Moira Elsley
French Toast with a Kick, p. 166: Bryan Larocque

Garlic-Onion Bites, p. 34: Mary Geale
Muskoka Blueberry Pie, p. 214: Ross Burwell
Napa Cabbage Salad, p. 118: Judy Anderson
Peaches & Raspberries in Wine, p. 208: Colleen
    Maloney-Arnold
Raspberry-Spinach Salad, p. 114: Peter O'Hare
Sandy's Orange Muffins, p. 192: Sandy Foster
Spicy Tortilla Wedges, p. 22: Nancy Weese
Stash-and-Go Sandwich, p. 156: Lynn Kennedy
Tabbouleh with a Twist, p. 109: Laura Robinson

Illustrations by Heather Holbrook

All photography (including cover) by Robert Wigington, except as noted below:

Suzanne McCormick: Fajitas, p. 49; Thai-Style
Wings, p. 57; Chicken Tikka, p. 61; Teriyaki Tuna,
p. 81; Orzo with Shrimp, p. 97; Chicken &
Sausage Jambalaya and Chicken & Black-Eyed
Peas, p. 129; Classic Gazpacho, p. 157; Spicy
Black Bean Soup, p. 160; Zucchini Frittata, p. 175;

Peach & Blueberry Shortcakes, p. 182 and
frontispiece; Baking Powder Biscuits, p. 201.

Olga Tracey: Marinated Stuffed Leg of Lamb,
p. 70; Pan-Fried Fish, pp. 170-171

Food styling by Ruth Gangbar and Jill Snider. Propping by Maggi Jones

Additional food styling by Claire Stancer and Debbi Charendoff Moses

TABLE OF CONTENTS

SUMMER WEEKEND COOKBOOK

CHAPTER CONTENTS:

You'll find a complete list of the recipes in each chapter, as well as menu suggestions and tips, at the start of each section.

Introduction

THE JOY OF SUMMER WEEKENDS – no alarm clock, no dash to fill your time slot in the bathroom, no listening to the morning news or traffic report. You open your eyes and savour the silence, broken only by birdsong. A delicious sunny day lies ahead.

Happy summer days invariably include good food. There is a problem, however: The cook wants to relax, too. All things considered, I would rather spend my weekend lazing on the deck with a good book than wrestling with grocery carts at the store, or dicing for hours in the kitchen.

This cookbook is designed to help you easily create wonderful-tasting food for your summer weekends. It's meant to provide you with ideas and inspiration for when you're entertaining relatives and friends, as well as when you're cooking just for the family. The focus is on relaxed, simple recipes that use fresh, seasonal ingredients. Many of the dishes can be made partly or entirely ahead so that last-minute fuss is kept to a minimum. (In fact, they taste even *better* when made in advance because the flavours are given time to develop.)

The recipes are also meant to be flexible: They can be varied to take advantage of what you've got on hand in the fridge and cupboards, and can often be expanded to accommodate last-minute unexpected appetites. They're very low-tech too, since many summer houses aren't equipped with all the conveniences of home. Although a food processor or blender will make preparation of some recipes easier, you can always substitute muscle power and a fork or potato masher. Because cooking outdoors is an essential part of summer, a good number of recipes rely on the grill. Not only does barbecuing help keep things cool inside, but the barbecue also becomes a focal point for

About Cottage Life magazine:

Each issue of *Cottage Life* magazine is packed with informative and entertaining reading to help you enjoy your time at your weekend retreat. Published 6 times a year, *Cottage Life* contains:

—maintenance and repair tips;
—sunny-day and rainy-day activities and games for kids and adults;
—do-it-yourself projects and practical "how-to" advice
—boating, watersports, nature, history, and humour
—and, of course, recipes and entertaining ideas like the ones in this book.

Enjoyable to read and lavishly illustrated, *Cottage Life* has received numerous awards, including Canada's "Magazine of the Year" award for overall excellence. For information on how to subscribe, contact:

Cottage Life, 111 Queen St. E., Ste. 408, Toronto, Ontario, Canada M5C 1S2; tel.: (416) 360-6880; fax: (416) 360-6814; e-mail: clmag@cottagelife.com

social activity. Friends gather around to review the day's events, plan what they're going to do tomorrow – and give advice to the cook, of course.

The recipes in this collection rely heavily on healthy fresh, seasonal vegetables and fruits, legumes, and grains – but there are some that are definitely special-occasion dishes. For sure, buttery corn bread and caramel-pecan sticky buns are not on the spa food list, but it is the weekend after all, and no-one needs to eat a *big* piece.

How to use this book

The recipes are divided into six sections: I. Appetizers, Starters, & Sundown Snacks; II. On the Barbecue; III. Salads & Side Dishes; IV. Make-Ahead Main Dishes, Pastas, & One-Pot Meals; V. Soups & Sandwiches; VI. Breakfast & Brunch; and VII. Baked Things & Desserts. At the start of each section, you'll find a complete list of the recipes included in that section, as well as menu and serving suggestions. The introduction at the start of each individual recipe and the tips at the end offer lots more ideas for putting together a fabulous meal. In addition to suggestions of what to serve the recipe with, they also provide variations and substitutions, and make-ahead tips.

Most of these recipes were first developed for *Cottage Life* magazine. I enjoy the support and enthusiastic, critical taste buds of the magazine's staff, and I am particularly grateful for the encouragement, meticulous eye, and exhortation to excellence provided by Ann Vanderhoof, the editor, and David Zimmer, the managing editor. (The latter, at 6'3", is my mentor on recipe yields.) A special thank you also goes to the readers of *Cottage Life* and the many friends who generously share their recipes and food ideas, particularly fellow food enthusiasts Kate Bush, Olga Truchan, Jennifer McLagan, and the great cooks at "All the Best." We also feast with our eyes, and I hope the brilliant mouth-watering photography of Bob Wigington and the appetizing design of the pages by Steve Manley will bring you as much pleasure as they bring me.

I hope your summer weekends are long and lovely, and filled with good friends and good food. Enjoy the book.

—*Jane Rodmell*

Stocking the Cupboard

After years of leaving the city on weekends with a hastily gathered collection of odd cans and packages, I have developed a few strategies that make it possible to enjoy good food on summer weekends with a minimum of anxiety and effort. The trick is in stocking the kitchen cupboards. With some basics in place, it's easier to whip up delicious spur-of-the-moment meals, cope with last-minute guests, and still have time to enjoy the sunshine. Here are some of the ingredients that are useful to have on hand for preparing the recipes in this book:

Herbs and spices

Many kitchen cupboards – especially those at seasonal places – contain jars of dried herbs and spices that have been around for years, if not generations. This summer, throw out the old and get new; you'll be surprised at the difference in taste. For better flavour, buy your herbs in leaf form rather than ground, then crumble them as you add to a dish. Better still, plant a few favourite herbs in pots, so they're on hand fresh when you need them.

The following herbs and spices are used in the recipes in this book (see also "The Spicy Cupboard," p. 14):

Dried: bay leaves, basil, black peppercorns, cayenne, cinnamon, cumin (seeds and ground), curry powder, dry mustard, oregano, paprika, rosemary, thyme, and salt; occasionally called for: allspice, cloves, coriander seed (ground), ginger, nutmeg, sesame seeds, and turmeric.

Fresh: basil, coriander (also known as cilantro), and flat-leaf parsley (also known as Italian parsley); occasionally called for: chives, dill, mint, oregano, tarragon, and thyme.

TIPS:

• Nothing replaces the flavour of fresh garlic, but the next best thing is chopped garlic preserved in oil. Sold in jars, it's a good emergency provision to have in the cottage or country pantry – and a much better alternative than powdered garlic or garlic salt, which usually have a very noticeable "artificial" taste.

• Fresh ginger root will keep for months if peeled, covered with sherry, and stored in a small jar in the fridge.

Canned foods

Every family has its favourites, but I find it particularly helpful to have the following cans in the cupboard:

At the top of my list is canned seafood – crab, tuna, salmon, clams, smoked oysters, anchovies, and shrimp. They can be used to make a spread or hors d'oeuvres for cocktail hour, turn a salad into a main dish, or provide the basis of a quick pasta sauce. Canned beans are also extremely handy – they can be added to salads and main dishes, or turned into a tasty dip. Stock a variety: red and white kidney beans, pinto beans, chick peas, black beans, black-eyed peas, and lentils. Rinse canned beans thoroughly before using to remove the preserving liquid.

Other useful cans and jars for the recipes in this book include: plum tomatoes, tomato paste, and plain tomato sauce (not the highly seasoned ready-to-eat variety); green and black olives in brine, oil-cured black olives, and pimiento-stuffed green olives (avoid canned, pitted black olives – usually from California – which often have an unpleasant soapy taste due to harsh processing methods); marinated and plain artichoke hearts; pimientos; capers; salsas (with several degrees of heat); water chestnuts; and peanut butter (chunky and smooth).

Condiments

While you can get by with a light vegetable oil, olive oil, and red and white wine vinegars for most of the recipes here, an assortment of oils and vinegars is a worthwhile investment. Sesame oil (for Oriental-flavoured dishes), balsamic vinegar, rice vinegar, and cider vinegar are all good additions to the cupboard shelves. Other condiments to have on hand include: Dijon mustard, Russian-style sweet or honey mustard, mayonnaise, horseradish, maple syrup, honey, sun-dried tomatoes, Worcestershire sauce, and soy sauce.

Other staples

A supply of pasta is essential. Good-quality dried pasta, made from durum wheat, has excellent flavour and texture, and blends with sauces much better than most commercially made "fresh" pasta. It keeps well and is available

TIPS:

• A couple of well-chosen jars in the cupboard can serve as the basis for instant emergency hors d'oeuvres. Excellent home-made style antipastos and spicy salsas are available ready-prepared. So too is tapenade (black olive paste) and roasted eggplant caviar (also known as "poor man's caviar"). All you have to do is find the crackers and open the jar when guests arrive unexpectedly.

• If you worry about whether the power has been out at your cottage while you weren't there (meaning the food in the freezer may have defrosted), try the following trick: Keep an ice cube in a small plastic container in the freezer. If, when you return, it has kept its shape, you can be sure the unit has been in constant operation. If the cube has melted and turned into a frozen puddle, it's wise to throw away the food stored in the freezer and fridge.

TIPS:

• While unopened cans and jars will keep quite well in the pantry, many items – even so-called "shelf-stable" foods like flour, nuts, and dry cereals – will deteriorate over time. To maximize shelf life (and to keep out pests), transfer boxed and bagged foods to clean, dry glass or plastic containers with well-fitting lids, label them, and store them in a cool, dry cupboard. And don't go overboard: Buy in quantities and sizes you will use within a month or two.

• Parmesan cheese will stay fresher if you buy it in a chunk and grate it as necessary.

• Some of the recipes in this book call for "deli-style cream cheese." This refers to the type sold in bulk and scooped into plastic containers. Not only does it taste better than the packaged kind sold in blocks, but it also spreads and blends more easily.

• Compile a list of the essentials in your cupboards and make photocopies of it. Use a copy to check supplies every week or so, then take it with you to the store. It's much easier (and more reliable) than trying to remember what you're out of after you're back in the city.

in so many different forms that the meal possibilities are endless. In addition to spaghetti, penne, and rotini, I like to have orzo (a rice-shaped pasta), rice noodles, and egg noodles on hand. Grains such as bulgur, couscous, and rice (long-grain and brown) are great for making salads, as are dried lentils and dried beans (instead of, or in addition to, the canned varieties). Good-quality chicken, beef, and vegetable stock cubes are a time-saving alternative to home-made stock.

Even if you're not much of a baker, it's well worth having a few baking supplies: all-purpose flour, instant yeast, baking powder, baking soda, cocoa, oats, corn meal, cornstarch, skim-milk powder, white and brown sugar, icing sugar, unsweetened chocolate squares, semi-sweet chocolate (chips and chunks), nuts, raisins (and other dried fruit), and vanilla. It's nice to know that if it rains all day, *someone* can whip up a batch of cookies or a loaf of bread. Also, you never know when you'll be confronted with a birthday and need to come up with a cake. (Make sure you tuck away a package of birthday candles!) Since yeast and baking powder lose their leavening power over time, replace them fresh every year.

With these items in the cupboard, and garlic, onions, lemons, and limes on hand, you have the basics in place for most of the recipes in this book. Just add the meat, fish, seasonal produce, cheese, and dairy items for your selected menu, and you're ready for the weekend. And don't forget the bread and milk!

The Spicy Cupboard

CHILE PEPPER PURÉE:

Handy to have to add to soups, salad dressings, salsas, mayonnaise, chili, and stews. It's excellent made with canned chipotle chiles, but you can experiment with dried anchos, New Mexico reds, and other types. This purée will keep in a covered jar in the refrigerator for about 2 weeks; it also freezes well.

1. With dried chiles, remove stems and shake out seeds from a good handful of chiles. Cover with boiling water and let stand for 30 minutes. Drain, reserving liquid, and purée, adding a tablespoon or two of vegetable oil (15–30 ml) and enough of the reserved soaking liquid so that the mixture has about the same consistency as tomato paste. Makes about 1/3–1/2 cup (75–125 ml).

2. With canned chipotle peppers in adobo, blend the contents of the can with a couple of tablespoons of vegetable oil and a squeeze of lemon or lime juice to make a smooth purée.

This book includes some spicy recipes – but none of them is fiery hot. If you follow the quantities given, you'll end up with a modest degree of heat. Adjust the recipe to your own taste by increasing or decreasing the amount of "hot" ingredients called for.

Here's the hot stuff you'll need to have on hand for the recipes in this book:

Basics

A bottle or two of hot sauce: Essentially a combination of peppers and vinegar (and/or citrus juice) in liquid form, it sometimes also contains onions, garlic, and carrots. Tabasco is probably the best known, but there are now countless brands on the market, with varying degrees of heat.

Hot red chile flakes: Buy them in a jar or at a bulk-food store, or make your own. (See the facing page.)

Fresh hot chile peppers or canned/jarred ones: Jalapeños are probably the most readily available fresh hot chile peppers and the type usually called for in this book. They are also available in jars or cans (as are mild green chiles), a handy substitute when you don't have fresh.

Chili powder: Beware of commercial chili powder that is a blend of ground chile peppers, oregano, cumin, salt, and garlic, sometimes with a corn-flour filler – especially if it has been at the back of your cupboard for a season or more. Look for a blend that includes only ground chile pepper, oregano, and cumin. Buy it in small quantities and use it while it's fresh. Better yet, experiment with pure ground chile powder, available in stores specializing in Mexican or Indian foods.

Extras:

Chinese chili sauce: Available in jars in Oriental markets, it's a useful condiment to have on hand to add zing to marinades, dressings, and sauces.

Dried whole chiles: Specialty markets often carry a number of different varieties. Dried ancho chiles are richly aromatic rather than hot; New Mexico reds are a little hotter. Chipotles (also spelled "chilpotles") are smoked jalapeños that add heat and a lovely smoky flavour. The dried chiles can be used to make your own chile flakes, chile powder, or chile purée. (See facing page and below.)

Chipotle peppers in adobo sauce: Although they are sold dried, these smoked jalapeño peppers are a little easier to find in cans, packed in a rich tomato sauce. (Look on the Mexican food shelf of the supermarket, or in a store specializing in Latin American foods.) You can chop or purée them and add to a variety of tomato-based stews and sauces, egg dishes, or marinades.

To make your own chile flakes or powder from dried chiles:

Toast the dried chiles on a baking tray in a 250°F (120°C) oven for 3–4 minutes. Remove stem, core, ribs, and seeds. Tear the flesh into pieces and leave to cool. Chop the chile pieces into flakes in a food processor, using on/off pulses. Or grind to a powder using a food processor, blender, or spice mill. Store your chile flakes or powder in a tightly sealed container in a cool, dark place so it will retain its freshness.

To prepare fresh chiles:

Broil them until their skin browns and blisters. Then place them in a paper bag or in a bowl covered with a towel and leave them to steam. Remove skin, stem, seeds, and ribs, and chop. Can be frozen for later use.

TIPS:

• Much of a chile's heat is in its seeds and ribs; if you like your food seriously hot, leave in a few of the seeds; otherwise, remove them. With all chiles, however, the heat will vary from pepper to pepper, so taste the dish after you have added a portion of the chiles.

• If you have sensitive skin, wear rubber gloves when handling chiles, and keep your hands away from your eyes and other sensitive areas. The volatile oils in the chiles can cause painful burns.

Entertaining a Crowd

The plates don't match, we regularly run out of wine glasses and forks, and there's never enough room for everyone to squeeze around the old pine table in the kitchen when the mosquitoes drive us indoors. But none of that matters. Some of the happiest times of summer are when a big group of friends and family gathers at our place on the lake. The days are long, the company is great, and the food tastes wonderful.

However, a certain amount of planning is essential. If the bread, beer, or snacks run out and the nearest store is an hour's drive (or boat trip) away, the chief cook may develop a nervous headache – or, worse, quit. The best strategy is to keep things simple, make a list, and delegate. First, nail down the vital statistics: how many meals, how many people? Are your guests young, old, or somewhere in between? (Teenagers will *dramatically* affect the quantity and type of food consumed.) Are there any special dietary requirements? Are there vegetarians in the group, for instance, or someone with a food allergy?

Next, the big question: What are you going to serve? That's where this book comes in. Take a look at the table of contents at the start of each recipe section for inspiration. You'll also find "crowd pleaser" suggestions in some of these tables of contents, while the introductions at the start of each recipe will provide you with more menu ideas; almost all the recipes can be easily multiplied to serve a crowd.

Good friends always ask what they can contribute. Accept their generous offer instantly, describe your general game plan, and make some suggestions. (It's the only way to avoid having four desserts, 12 quarts of green beans, and no lettuce.) If there is a non-cook in the crowd, an always-appreciated con-

TIPS:

• When entertaining a crowd, always have a couple of coolers on hand, as there's never enough room in the fridge. (Ask guests to bring one along, with a couple of bags of ice.) Use them to hold pop, beer, and wine, or even the fixings for breakfast until they're needed.

• To avoid the hassle of mixing individual drinks when you've got a crowd, serve drinks that can be mixed in batches and served from a jug or punch bowl – Bloody Marys or Caesars, sangría, or margaritas, for instance.

• Try to plan your shopping and menus for the weekend so that things go together and so that leftovers from one meal can be incorporated into a snack or salad the following day. You'll then not be faced with a zillion small containers or packages that need to be transported back to the city.

tribution is some extra beer, pop, or wine. (We never seem to pack enough, perhaps because it takes up so much room in the car.) We never seem to bring enough bread, either. If the gathering is in the country, suggest someone stop at a city bakery before leaving town, or detour to a great little bakery on the way. Or recommend one of your guests pull in at a farmers' market or vegetable stand en route to get fresh corn or field tomatoes to serve with the barbecue dinner, or blueberries to go in the pancakes at breakfast.

As dinner time approaches, work out a strategy. Sometimes the whole group gets involved: Drinks are handed round, suitable music is selected, and everyone gets to work shucking corn, snipping beans, making the salad, setting the table. When a crowd gathers around the barbecue, as it inevitably does, designate a chef to take care of the basting and turning and to mastermind the timing of the operation.

At other times at our summer place, there is division of labour: One group of helpers joins in the preparation of the meal, but afterwards they sit and enjoy the sunset while the rest of the group gets into gear and does the cleanup.

Another strategy when the numbers increase is to divide up responsibility for meals. For instance, a family or group may take on Saturday night supper – right from the shopping through the cooking and including the cleanup – while another group handles Sunday brunch. One memorable weekend, a thoughtful friend volunteered to bring along all the sundown snacks. What a feast – all kinds of new and wonderful tastes; we hardly needed supper.

And remember, above all, relax and have fun: Time spent with family and friends on summer weekends should be savoured.

TIPS:

• Keep in mind that your barbecue has limited capacity. If the grill is going to be full of chicken or ribs, plan vegetables that can be done inside on the stove. Or, better still, serve salads with the main dish, since they can be prepared ahead and keep stove use to a minimum. If you've got a *really* big crowd, to ensure everyone (including the cook) gets to eat at once, borrow an extra barbecue from a neighbour or even rent a big charcoal "steel-drum" style grill.

• Specific suggestions for preparing breakfast for a crowd can be found on pp. 164, 166, 168, and 172.

• Never refuse an offer to help with the washing up.

I. APPETIZERS, STARTERS, & SUNDOWN SNACKS

For Heartier Appetites

Sometimes the happy hour calls for something a little more substantial – especially if it's going to extend into dinner. These recipes, which you'll find in other sections of the book, will nicely fill the bill:

Artichoke Dip

1 clove	garlic, *finely minced*	
1 tbsp	onion, *grated*	15 ml
1 cup	mayonnaise	250 ml
¼ tsp	cayenne	1 ml
2 tbsp	Parmesan cheese, *grated*	30 ml
	salt and white pepper	
1 can	artichoke hearts *(14 oz/398 ml)*	
	paprika	
	pita bread, *cut into triangles and toasted*	

TIPS:

• The flavour of canned artichokes improves greatly if you drain them, rinse them under cold water, and drain them again.

• Be sure to use plain canned artichoke hearts in this recipe – not the marinated ones that come in jars.

This decadent dip has made an appearance at many gatherings. Friends will gasp and say it's too rich and they shouldn't have anymore – and then it will be all gone!

1. Thoroughly blend the first 5 ingredients together. Season to taste.

2. Rinse and drain the artichokes and chop into small pieces. Stir into mayonnaise mixture.

3. Spoon into an ovenproof bowl or gratin dish of about 2-cup (500-ml) capacity, sprinkle with paprika, and bake at 350°F (180°C) for 15–20 minutes, until the dip is bubbling and the top is beginning to brown. Serve hot with pita bread crisps.

Makes 2 cups (500 ml).

 QUICK TRICK:
For an easy antipasto salad, cut canned artichoke hearts into quarters and combine with chopped red onion, celery, and black olives. Toss with a dressing made from oilve oil, wine vinegar, garlic, and hot red pepper flakes. Sprinkle with lots of chopped fresh parsley and paprika. Serve with crisp toasts.

Layered Black Bean Dip

2 cups	cooked black beans *(1 19-oz/540-ml can)*	500 ml
8 oz	cream cheese	250 g
2 cloves	garlic, *minced*	
2 tbsp	lime juice	30 ml
1 tsp	lime zest, *grated*	5 ml
dash	hot sauce, *or to taste*	
	salt	
2	large tomatoes, *peeled, seeded, and chopped*	
1 cup	old Cheddar cheese, *grated*	250 ml
4	green onions, *finely chopped*	
¼ cup	black olives, *pitted and chopped*	60 ml
1 tbsp	jalapeño peppers, *finely chopped*	15 ml
½ cup	sour cream	125 ml

This Mexican-inspired dish makes a great party plate – it's wonderfully easy, makes a lot, and is open to variation. If you don't have one of the ingredients on hand, you can leave it out or substitute something else. (See Tips, below.) The trick is simply to have several layers/rings of contrasting flavours, colours, and textures. Serve with baskets of tortilla chips for dipping.

1. Blend together black beans, cream cheese, garlic, lime juice and zest, hot sauce, and salt to taste. A blender or food processor does the job in seconds, but an old-fashioned potato masher works too.

2. Spread black bean mixture on a large platter. Arrange a wide ring of chopped tomatoes on top around the edge; spread grated cheese in a ring inside that, followed by a ring of the green onions, followed by the olives and jalapeños combined. Put sour cream in the centre.

Serves a bunch.

TIPS:

• Canned black beans are available in large urban supermarkets, or you can cook your own. (Instructions on p. 110.)

• Instead of the base of black beans, use plain cream cheese. Or heat a can (14 oz/398 ml) of refried beans and use that as the base. (Warm the platter first.)

• Add a ring of chopped avocado or a layer of guacamole. (Recipe on p. 25.)

Spicy Tortilla Wedges

6	**medium flour tortillas** *(8"/20 cm)*	
½ cup	**salsa**	125 ml
1	**large tomato,** *seeded and chopped*	
2	**green onions,** *finely chopped*	
1 tbsp	**jalapeño peppers,** *finely chopped (fresh or from a jar)*	15 ml
1 cup	**Cheddar cheese,** *grated*	250 ml
1 cup	**feta cheese,** *crumbled*	250 ml
1	**egg,** *lightly beaten*	
¼ cup	**black olives,** *pitted and chopped*	60 ml

These easy-to-make gourmet grilled cheese sandwiches cook on the barbecue in minutes.

1. Place 3 tortillas flat on work surface. Cover each of these tortillas with a thin layer of salsa.

2. Combine remaining ingredients and mix well. Spread ⅓ of the mixture on top of the salsa on each tortilla. Top each with one of the remaining tortillas to cover filling.

3. Grill over medium-high heat for 8–10 minutes, turning halfway through (you'll need 2 spatulas), until tortillas are lightly browned and cheese has melted. Remove and cut into wedges.

Makes 18–24 pieces.

TIPS:

• Tortillas are available in the refrigerator or freezer section of many supermarkets; keep a package or two in your freezer – they're a good base for many pre-supper snacks. (Also see recipes on pages 29, 34, and 35.)

• These wedges can also be done in the oven. Place tortillas on baking sheets and bake at 350°F (180°C) for about 10 minutes, until the cheese melts.

The filling for these spicy tortillas can be assembled quickly, and they cook in 10 minutes on the barbecue or in the oven. Serve with plenty of napkins.

Caponata

6 tbsp	**olive oil**	90 ml
2	**young globe eggplants,** *about 1½ lbs (750 g) in total, cut in ¾" (2-cm) cubes*	
3 stalks	**celery,** *trimmed and thinly sliced*	
1	**medium onion,** *thinly sliced*	
1½ cups	**tomato sauce** *or* **puréed canned plum tomatoes**	375 ml
dash	**sugar** *(if necessary)*	
	salt and freshly ground pepper	
2 tbsp	**capers,** *rinsed and drained*	30 ml
½ cup	**black olives,** *halved and pitted*	125 ml
3 tbsp	**balsamic** *or* **red wine vinegar** *(or to taste)*	45 ml
	fresh flat-leaf parsley, *chopped*	

This robust Sicilian dish combines the rich, earthy flavours of eggplant and olives with sharp capers. Serve with crisp toasts on its own, or make it part of an antipasto platter. It also makes a good side dish served with grilled fish or meat.

1. Heat 3 tbsp (45 ml) of the oil in a large, heavy skillet. Add eggplant and cook over medium heat until lightly browned (about 7 minutes), turning often. (Cook in 2 batches if necessary.) Set aside on paper towel to drain.

2. Heat 1½ tbsp (20 ml) of the oil in the skillet; add celery and cook until tender. Set aside on paper towel.

3. Heat remaining oil, add onion, and cook until soft. Stir in tomatoes. Season with salt, pepper, and a dash of sugar (if needed), and simmer for 5 minutes. Return celery to pan, and add capers, olives, and vinegar. Simmer for 15 minutes. Return eggplant to pan, and simmer for 10 minutes.

4. Turn out into a bowl, cover, and set aside to cool and for flavours to develop. Taste and adjust seasoning before serving. Serve at room temperature with a garnish of fresh parsley.

Makes about 4 cups (1 L).

TIPS:

• This is a great make-ahead appetizer, as it tastes even better after it has had a chance to sit overnight. Will keep about a week in the fridge.

• Young, small eggplants and Japanese eggplants have tender skin, so it's not necessary to peel them. Large eggplants should be peeled and the cubes sprinkled with a teaspoon of salt and allowed to drain in a colander for an hour to draw out the bitter juices. Rinse and pat dry.

Guacamole

2	**large ripe avocados**
	juice of 1 lime *or* **½ lemon**
1–2 cloves	**garlic,** *finely chopped*
2 tbsp	**onion,** *finely chopped* **30 ml**
1	**ripe tomato,** *peeled, seeded, and chopped*
1–2	**fresh jalapeño peppers,** *seeded, and chopped*
1 tbsp	**fresh coriander,** *finely chopped* **15 ml**
pinch	**cayenne** *or* **a few drops of hot sauce**
	salt

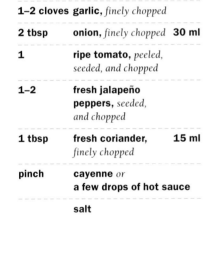

A tasty dip by itself with corn chips, guacamole is also an essential topping for Steak Fajitas (p. 48) and Mexican Burgers (p. 73). It can also be turned into a delicious spread for crackers by blending it with deli-style cream cheese.

1. Halve avocados, remove pits, and scoop flesh from the skins. Sprinkle with lemon or lime juice (peeled avocado quickly turns brown when exposed to air, and lemon or lime juice retards this process) and mash with a fork; don't make the mixture too smooth.

2. Combine remaining ingredients in a small bowl. Stir half of this mixture into the mashed avocado. Taste and adjust seasoning, adding a dash more lemon or lime juice if necessary. Garnish with the remainder of the garlic, onion, and tomato mixture.

Makes about 1½ cups (375 ml).

TIPS:

• If you don't have any fresh jalapeños on hand, you can substitute ones from a jar, or a couple more healthy dashes of hot sauce.

• You can omit the coriander – the taste will be somewhat different, but delicious nonetheless.

• Guacamole tastes best when freshly made, so serve within an hour or two of making; an occasional stir keeps the colour fresh.

• To test an avocado for ripeness, gently stick a toothpick in the stem end; it should slip smoothly in and out.

Barbecued Marinated Brie

1 tbsp	lemon juice	15 ml
1 tbsp	vegetable oil	15 ml
½	red pepper, *finely chopped*	
1 tbsp	fresh parsley, *finely chopped*	15 ml
1 clove	garlic, *minced*	
1 tsp	Dijon mustard	5 ml
¼ tsp	black pepper	1 ml
8-oz wheel	Brie *or* Camembert	250 g
	crackers *or* French bread	

Not only is this appetizer delicious, it looks fabulous too. And it's a perfect starter when you have the barbecue going to cook the main course.

1. Combine all ingredients except cheese and bread or crackers. Mix well.

2. Place cheese wheel in a small, shallow glass dish and poke it full of holes with a fork. Pour marinade over cheese. Cover and let sit in refrigerator at least 2 hours, or overnight.

3. Preheat barbecue to medium (350°F/180°C). Place a piece of foil on grill and poke holes in foil with a skewer. Place cheese on foil.

4. Heat just until cheese starts to bulge around the edges and centre is soft, about 15 minutes. Serve warm with crackers or French bread.

Makes about 8 servings.

TIPS:

• For a colourful presentation, use a combination of red and green peppers. (Or just substitute half a green pepper, if that's what you've got on hand.)

• The Brie can also be heated in the oven: Bake at 350°F (180°C) for 10–15 minutes, until cheese just starts to bulge around edges.

Marinate the Brie the day before serving. Then you just have to heat the cheese on the grill and put out a basket of crackers when you're ready to serve.

Chile con Queso

3 tbsp	olive oil	45 ml
1	**medium onion,** *finely chopped*	
4	**green onions,** *finely chopped*	
1–3	**jalapeño peppers,** *finely chopped*	
½	**sweet red pepper,** *finely chopped*	
2 cloves	**garlic,** *finely chopped*	
2	**large ripe tomatoes,** *peeled, seeded, and chopped* **or**	
1½ cups	**canned tomatoes,** *well drained and chopped*	375 ml
	salt and freshly ground pepper	
¼ cup	35% cream	60 ml
1 lb	**Cheddar cheese,** *grated (use half mild, half sharp)*	500 g
2 tbsp	flour	30 ml
1 tsp	ground cumin	5 ml

A hot Mexican-style cheese dip for dunking corn chips, pieces of grilled sausage, or crunchy fresh vegetables. Adjust the number of hot peppers to your taste.

1. Heat oil in a heavy pot over moderate heat, add onions and peppers, and cook until soft.

2. Stir in tomatoes, garlic, salt, and pepper; simmer for about 5 minutes, until liquid is evaporated. Add cream.

3. Toss grated cheese with flour and cumin. Gradually add to the hot tomato-cream mixture, stirring constantly over moderate heat until sauce is smooth. Serve warm and surround with corn chips and other interesting things for dipping.

Makes about 3 cups (750 ml).

QUICK TRICK:
If olives straight out of the jar don't seem to have enough pizzazz for cocktail hour, toss them with a teaspoon or so of chile flakes, a couple of cloves of sliced garlic, a little olive oil, dried oregano, and a chopped roasted red pepper. Set aside for an hour or so for flavours to blend. Olives will keep for a week or more in the refrigerator.

Smoked Salmon Spirals

8 oz	deli-style cream cheese	250 g
2 tbsp	Russian-style sweet mustard	30 ml
1 tbsp	sour cream *or* mayonnaise	15 ml
4	large flour tortillas *(10"/25 cm)*	
12 oz	smoked salmon, *thinly sliced*	375 g
2 tbsp	fresh dill, *chopped*	30 ml
2 tbsp	fresh chives, *chopped*	30 ml
	freshly ground pepper	
8 leaves	Boston lettuce *or* fresh spinach, *washed and thoroughly dried*	

"This is one of the most popular appetizers I make in my classes," says Toronto cooking teacher and food writer Bonnie Stern, the creator of this recipe – and I can bear out the truth of that remark. Perfect for parties, these spirals are easy to make and very tasty.

1. Cream together cream cheese, mustard, and sour cream or mayonnaise.

2. Lay tortillas flat on a work surface and spread each evenly with cheese mixture. Lay salmon slices in a single layer on top, leaving a 1" (2-cm) border at the top covered just with cheese, so that the rolls will stick together. Sprinkle salmon with dill, chives, and pepper. Arrange lettuce or spinach leaves on top.

3. Roll tortillas up tightly, pressing firmly to seal. Wrap in plastic wrap and refrigerate an hour or two.

4. Trim off raggedy ends of tortilla rolls, then cut each roll into 8–10 slices on the diagonal.

Makes about 32–40 bites.

TIPS:

• This basic technique can be used with a variety of fillings. Try topping the cream cheese mixture with thinly sliced cucumber and finely chopped cooked shrimp. Or use thinly sliced spicy salami, omitting the dill or substituting chopped fresh basil.

• The rolls can be made up to a day ahead. Use fresh spinach leaves instead of lettuce – they hold up better.

• For a light version, use low-fat cream cheese or yoghurt cheese, and replace the sour cream or mayonnaise with yoghurt.

Chile & Cheese Squares

cut 1" slices.

½ loaf	**French bread**	
1 can	**evaporated milk** *(12 oz/385 ml)*	
~~4~~ 3 cans	**mild green chiles,** *chopped* *(4.5 oz/127 ml)*	
2 cups	**old Cheddar cheese,** *grated*	500 ml
2 cups	**Monterey Jack cheese,** *grated*	500 ml
4	**eggs**	

An ideal cottage appetizer: It tastes great, is easy to make, and can be prepared ahead, then simply reheated to serve.

1. Cut bread on the diagonal into ½" (1-cm) slices. ~~Dip slices into about ⅔ cup (150 ml) of the evaporated milk, then gently press out as much liquid as possible~~.

2. Arrange the bread slices in a single layer in the bottom of a lightly buttered 9" x 13" (23-cm x 33-cm) baking dish. Spread half the chiles evenly on top. Sprinkle with Cheddar, spread remaining chiles on top, then sprinkle with Monterey Jack.

3. Beat eggs and ⅔ cup (150 ml) of evaporated milk together to blend. Pour evenly over filling.

4. Bake at 350°F (180°C) for 35–40 minutes, or until set and light golden. Cool 5 minutes, then cut into small squares. Serve warm.

Makes about 50 squares.

TIPS:

• To prepare ahead, bake as above, cool, and cut into squares. When ready to serve, reheat at 350°F (180°C) about 5 minutes, or until hot.

• Add zip by mixing chopped jalapeño peppers with the mild green chiles.

30

Roasted Eggplant Caviar

1	globe eggplant, *(about 1 lb/500 g)*	
3 tbsp	olive oil	45 ml
4 cloves	garlic, *unpeeled*	
½	small red onion, *sliced but unpeeled*	
1 tsp	balsamic vinegar	5 ml
squeeze	lemon juice	
	salt and freshly ground pepper	
	fresh parsley and ripe olives, *chopped (for garnish)*	

TIP:

• The eggplant, garlic, and onion can also be roasted on the barbecue. See p. 90 for directions.

This simple purée of roasted eggplant makes a wonderful snack with sesame crackers or wedges of pita bread.

1. Slice eggplant in half lengthwise and brush cut surfaces with olive oil. Place cut side down on a lightly oiled baking sheet.

2. Arrange garlic cloves and onion slices on the sheet, and brush with oil. Bake in a preheated 375°F (190°C) oven for about 35 minutes until vegetables are tender.

3. Place eggplant in a colander to drain and, when cool enough to handle, peel away the skin in strips starting at the stem end. Snip the tips from the garlic cloves and squeeze out the roasted garlic. Remove outer skin from roasted onion slices.

4. Using a food processor or a potato masher, purée the eggplant, garlic, and onion, adding the rest of the oil (a tablespoon or so), the balsamic vinegar, a squeeze of lemon juice, and salt and pepper to taste. Set aside, covered, for an hour or so to let the flavour develop.

Makes about 1½ cups (375 ml).

Smoked Trout Spread

6 oz	**deli-style cream cheese**	**175 g**
8 oz	**smoked trout**	**250 g**
2 tbsp	**fresh dill,** *chopped*	**30 ml**
½–1 tbsp	**fresh lemon juice,** *to taste*	**10–15 ml**
1 tbsp	**capers,** *chopped*	**15 ml**
1 tsp	**prepared horseradish**	**5 ml**
pinch	**sugar**	
	salt and freshly ground pepper	

The area around my cottage is dotted with trout farms, many of which have their own smokehouse. Smoked trout is delicious for a special brunch, lunch, or happy-hour snack. This recipe turns the smoked fish into a tasty spread.

1. In a food processor, blend the cream cheese with the dill, lemon juice, capers, horseradish, and half the trout until smooth. (Or mash the ingredients together with a fork.)

2. Add the remaining trout and process (or mash) lightly to combine. Season to taste.

3. Serve on melba toast, slices of fresh pumpernickel bread, crisp cucumber rounds, or spears of Belgian endive.

Makes about 2 cups (500 ml).

QUICK TRICK:

Don't panic if you run out of crackers: Home-made melba toast is easy to make, and a nice change. Cut good stale bread – rye, pumpernickel, whole wheat, sourdough, challah, walnut bread, or even raisin bread – into thin slices. Spread on cookie sheets and bake at 300˚F (150˚C) until crisp (about 10 minutes). Or cut pita bread into triangles with scissors and toast in the oven. These pita chips are delicious brushed with garlic-flavoured olive oil and sprinkled with grated Parmesan cheese before toasting.

Herb & Garlic Dip

8 oz	**deli-style cream cheese**	250 g
2 tbsp	**sour cream** *or* **yoghurt**	30 ml
1–2 cloves	**garlic,** *minced*	
¼ cup	**green onions,** *finely chopped*	60 ml
2 tbsp	**dill,** *finely chopped*	30 ml
2 tbsp	**parsley,** *finely chopped*	30 ml
dash	**hot sauce**	
	salt and freshly ground pepper	
	assorted fresh vegetables	

The crisper usually can be relied on for a motley collection of vegetables: carrots, celery, sweet peppers, zucchini, mushrooms, cucumbers, cherry tomatoes. A plate of crudités and dip is easy to prepare – and always popular.

1. Combine cream cheese with sour cream or yoghurt, herbs, and spices, and season to taste. Leave in the refrigerator for a while for flavours to blend.

2. Clean and trim vegetables and cut into slivers or chunks to serve with dip.

Makes about 1¹/₂ cups (375 ml).

QUICK TRICK:

Here's the widely shared secret for the easiest vegetable or chip dip in the world: Simply combine one package of Knorr vegetable soup mix without noodles with 2 cups (500 ml) sour cream, or part sour cream and part yoghurt. Refrigerate for an hour or so to allow flavours to mingle.

TIP:

• For variety, omit the sour cream and add chopped seafood to turn the dip into a savoury spread. Drain canned shrimp, crab, or lobster well and chop finely. Or, if you happen to have a few ends of smoked salmon left over, you could add them instead, with a few chopped capers.

Garlic-Onion Bites

½ cup	mayonnaise	125 ml
½ cup	**Parmesan** *or* **Romano cheese,** *grated*	125 ml
½ cup	**Spanish, Vidalia,** *or* **red onion,** *chopped*	125 ml
¼ cup	**fresh basil,** *chopped* (*or 1 tbsp/15 ml dried*)	60 ml
4 cloves	**garlic,** *minced*	
	salt and freshly ground pepper	
4	**medium flour tortillas** (*8"/20 cm*) **or**	
1	**prepared pizza crust** (*12"/30 cm*)	
	olive oil	

Keep a container of the prepared topping in the refrigerator for a quick snack or instant appetizer.

1. Combine the first 5 ingredients in small bowl. Mix well. Season to taste with salt and pepper.

2. Brush tortillas or pizza crust lightly with olive oil.

3. Spread cheese mixture thinly and evenly over tortillas or crust.

4. Bake at 450°F (230°C) for 8–12 minutes, or until crust is crisp and golden and topping is hot. Cut into wedges.

Makes about 32 pieces (if made on tortillas).

TIPS:

• For tiny triangles, use 6" pizza crusts.

• Can also be done on the barbecue. Preheat barbecue, then cook on medium with lid closed until crust is crisp and topping is hot – about 5 minutes if using tortillas, longer if using pizza crust.

• Topping will keep at least 3 days in the fridge. Bring required amount to room temperature before using.

Crab Burrito Slices

8 oz	**cream cheese,** *at room temperature*	250 g
¾ cup	**red pepper,** *finely chopped*	175 ml
2	**green onions,** *finely chopped*	
3 tbsp	**fresh parsley,** *finely chopped*	45 ml
½ cup	**old Cheddar cheese,** *grated*	125 ml
½ tsp	**cayenne pepper**	2 ml
1 can	**crab meat,** *drained* *(4.2 oz/120 g)*	
5	**large flour tortillas** *(10"/25 cm)*	
	salsa	

Since the burritos store and travel well, this is a great hors d'oeuvre to prepare at home ahead of time and take with you on the weekend.

1. Beat cream cheese with a fork or wooden spoon until smooth.

2. Add red pepper, green onions, parsley, cheese, cayenne, and crab meat. Mix well.

3. Divide mixture equally between the tortillas. Spread evenly, then roll each tortilla up tightly. Wrap well in plastic and refrigerate for at least 1 hour or overnight.

4. When ready to serve, cut rolls into ¾" (2-cm) slices. Discard ends (or eat them yourself). Place slices on greased baking sheet.

5. Bake at 350°F (180°C) for about 10 minutes, or until heated through. Serve hot with salsa for dipping.

Makes about 40 pieces.

Keep a package or two of tortillas on hand for making these Garlic-Onion Bites and Crab Burrito Slices.

White Bean Dip

1 can	**white beans,** *rinsed and drained* (19 oz/540 ml)	
2 tbsp	**olive oil**	30 ml
2 tbsp	**onion,** *finely chopped*	30 ml
1 tsp	**garlic,** *minced*	5 ml
½ tsp	**ground cumin**	2 ml
1 tsp	**chile powder**	5 ml
½ tsp	**hot sauce** *(or to taste)*	2 ml
1 tbsp	**lemon juice**	15 ml
	salt and freshly ground pepper	
	fresh coriander or parsley, *chopped* **or Cheddar cheese,** *grated (for garnish; optional)*	

A food processor allows you to combine the ingredients for a tasty dip in seconds, but failing that, a potato masher and a sharp knife will do the job. Serve this dip warm or at room temperature with warm taco chips, wedges of toasted pita bread, or an assortment of crisp raw vegetables.

1. Mash beans or purée in food processor.

2. Heat oil in small pan, add onion and garlic, and cook until soft. Add spices and stir briefly over moderate heat. Combine this mixture with the puréed beans.

3. Add hot sauce, lemon juice, and salt and pepper to taste.

4. Garnish with chopped coriander or parsley, or a sprinkling of grated Cheddar cheese.

Makes about 1½ cups (375 ml).

TIPS:

• Before using canned beans or canned chickpeas, rinse under cold water and drain well to remove the preserving liquid.

• Substitute other varieties of beans depending on what you have in the cupboard – black beans or red kidney beans, for instance.

Crab Toasts

1 can	**snow crab meat,** *well drained (4.2 oz/120 g)*	
2	**green onions,** *finely chopped*	
1 clove	**garlic,** *finely chopped*	
¼ cup	**mayonnaise**	**60 ml**
2 tbsp	**lemon juice**	**30 ml**
1 tbsp	**fresh parsley,** *chopped*	**15 ml**
2–3 dashes hot sauce		
	salt and freshly ground pepper	
1	**egg white**	
1 tbsp	**melted butter**	**15 ml**
3 slices	**whole-wheat** *or* **homemade-style white bread**	

Sometimes an occasion requires a fancier snack. While this recipe uses crab, you can substitute other kinds of canned (or fresh) seafood – shrimp or lobster, for example – with marvellous results.

1. Combine crab meat with green onions, garlic, mayonnaise, lemon juice, parsley, and hot sauce and season to taste.

2. Beat egg white until stiff, and fold lightly into crab mixture.

3. Trim crusts from bread and cut into serving-size squares or fingers. Place on a baking sheet and set in a 350°F (180°C) oven for a few minutes until lightly crisped.

4. Spread crab mixture on the toasts. Brush the tops lightly with melted butter and set under the broiler until crab topping puffs and browns lightly. Serve hot.

Makes 12–18 pieces.

TIPS:

• Steps 1–3 can be done the day before serving.

• If you're particularly ambitious (and not worried about fat), you can deep-fry the toasts instead of broiling them, which gives them a lovely crunchy exterior.

• For an interesting variation, omit the egg white and use the mixture as a sandwich filling, or stuff it into miniature pita pockets and serve as an hors d'oeuvre.

Mozzarella Bruschetta

1 loaf	**Italian-style bread** *or* **French baguette**
	olive oil
1 clove	**garlic**
	fresh basil, *chopped* *(optional)*

Marinated Mozzarella

¹⁄₂ lb	**mozzarella**	**250 g**
3 tbsp	**olive oil**	**45 ml**
1	**sun-dried tomato,** *cut in slivers*	
1 tbsp	**Herbes de Provence** *or* **a mix of equal parts dried basil, oregano, and thyme**	**15 ml**
1 tsp	**garlic,** *finely chopped*	**5 ml**
¹⁄₄ tsp	**hot red pepper flakes**	**1 ml**
	salt and freshly ground pepper	

TIP:
• For a different flavour, substitute bocconcini (young, fresh mozzarella) or mild goat cheese.

There are endless variations on the theme of bruschetta, essentially crisp slices of bread with flavourful toppings. Even at its simplest – with chopped fresh tomato and onion, Parmesan cheese, and a scattering of herbs, as shown here – bruschetta makes a popular snack, but try it with Marinated Mozzarella for a delicious alternative.

1. Cut mozzarella into small cubes and toss with oil and seasonings. Although the cheese may be used right away, the flavour will improve if you let it stand at least an hour in the refrigerator.

2. Cut the baguette in half lengthwise, or cut chunky slices of Italian-style bread. Brush slices with olive oil and rub with a cut garlic clove. Season with salt and pepper, and toast lightly on the grill.

3. Top with cubes of Marinated Mozzarella and sprinkle with chopped basil if you like. Place slices on a metal tray and return to the grill or oven (375°F/190°C) for a few minutes until the cheese begins to melt. Serve hot, cut in serving-size wedges.

Serves 6.

TIP:
• Marinated Mozzarella also makes a good savoury snack all by itself, or it can be tossed in a salad or used on top of pizza. It will keep 2–3 days in the fridge.

Curried Nuts & Chile Nuts

2 cups	pecan halves	500 ml
2 cups	cashews	500 ml
2 cups	unblanched whole almonds	500 ml
¼ cup	melted butter	60 ml
	salt	

Curried Nuts

1 tsp	hot sauce	5 ml
4 tsp	curry powder	20 ml
2 cups	raisins	500 ml

Chile Nuts

½ tsp	hot sauce	2 ml
½ tsp	ground coriander	2 ml
½ tsp	paprika	2 ml
½ tsp	cumin	2 ml
½ tsp	cayenne	2 ml
½ tsp	freshly ground black pepper	2 ml
1½ tsp	Mexican chile powder	7 ml

These twists on standard salted nuts will appeal to people with a hot spot instead of a sweet tooth. Although the recipe calls for mixed nuts, of course you can stick to one type if you have a particular favourite.

1. Preheat oven to 300°F (150°C). Place nuts in a large bowl.

2. Combine butter with hot sauce and spices for either Curried Nuts or Chile Nuts. Pour mixture over nuts and toss to coat on all sides.

3. Spread nuts in a single layer on large baking sheets and bake for about 30 minutes, stirring now and again.

4. Sprinkle nuts with salt and transfer to trays lined with paper towel to cool. Add raisins to Curried Nuts. Package mixture in plastic bags or airtight containers. Allow flavours to develop overnight before serving.

Makes 8 cups (2 L) of Curried Nuts, 6 cups (1.5 L) of Chile Nuts.

TIP:

• Best eaten within a few days. If nuts are kept longer, they will regain their crispness if warmed in a low oven for a few minutes before serving.

Sweet & Spicy Nuts

2 tbsp	peanut oil	30 ml
2 cups	blanched whole almonds	500 ml
2 tsp	table sugar	10 ml
½ tsp	cumin	2 ml
1 tsp	cayenne *or* **hot sauce**	5 ml
	salt	

QUICK TRICK:
Freshly popped popcorn is always popular, but if plain popcorn seems ho-hum for cocktail hour, try tossing it with melted butter, a couple of shakes of grated Parmesan cheese, a spoonful of dried mixed herbs, and a couple of dashes of hot sauce.

Make up a batch or two of these hot almonds to have on hand for cocktail hour. They're best when freshly toasted, although they'll stay fresh in an airtight container for a week. (To keep them that long, though, you'll definitely have to hide the container at the back of the cupboard.)

1. Heat oil in a large, heavy skillet. Add almonds, sprinkle with sugar, and toss over medium-high heat until nuts are a light, even brown.

2. Turn out into a bowl and toss with cumin, cayenne, and salt.

3. Spread nuts on paper towel to cool and crisp. Store in an airtight tin.

Makes 2 cups (500 ml).

Salsa from the Cupboard

1 tbsp	vegetable oil	15 ml
1	small onion, *chopped*	
1 can	plum tomatoes, *drained, seeded, and roughly chopped* (28 oz/796 ml)	
3	green onions, *chopped*	
2 cloves	garlic, *minced*	
1–2 tbsp	jalapeño peppers, *finely chopped*	15–30 ml
½ tsp	oregano	2 ml
½ tsp	cumin	2 ml
dash	hot sauce	
2 tbsp	wine vinegar	30 ml
	salt and freshly ground pepper	
1 tbsp	fresh coriander *or* parsley, *chopped (optional)*	15 ml

A bowl of spicy salsa served with corn chips makes a great snack all by itself. But don't sell it short: It's an extremely useful condiment to have on hand, essential with Mexican and Tex-Mex recipes such as Huevos Rancheros (p. 173), Chicken Quesadillas (p. 150), and Steak Fajitas (p. 48). It's also delicious tucked into an omelette or served alongside grilled fish. There are many good bottled salsas on the market, but if you find yourself without one, this version is not only tasty but can be whipped up from ingredients you're likely to have in the cupboard.

1. Heat oil and gently soften onion. Add tomatoes and remaining ingredients. Simmer, stirring now and again, for 15 minutes.

2. Taste and adjust seasoning, making it a little hotter if you like. Transfer to a serving bowl and chill.

Makes about 2½ cups (625 ml).

TIPS:

• Fresh coriander is a herb with a distinctive musky flavour. If it is unavailable, substitute fresh parsley for a different taste or omit it altogether. (The flavour of coriander seed is unlike that of fresh coriander.)

• The salsa will keep in the refrigerator for about a week.

II. ON THE BARBECUE

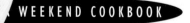

Texas Barbecued Brisket

3½ lbs	beef brisket *(approx.)*	1.5 kg
1/4 cup	oil	60 ml
2 tbsp	lemon juice	30 ml
2 cloves	**garlic,** *finely chopped*	
1 tsp	**each thyme, black pepper, paprika, cumin, and cayenne**	5 ml
	Tangy Texas Barbecue Sauce *(facing page),* or *your own favourite*	

BARBECUING TIP:

• Slow cooking in aromatic smoke is a delicious way to add intense flavour to large cuts of meat:

Soak wood chips in water for 30 minutes. Drain and, if you're using a charcoal grill, place directly on the charcoal. If you're using a gas grill, put the chips in a shallow aluminum pan with holes punched in the bottom and place the pan over the burner. (Don't throw wood chips directly onto the rocks or plates of a gas barbecue, as the ash can clog the gas jets.)

Use only hardwood chips, such as hickory or mesquite. For more delicate flavour, try maple, apple, or cherry wood; grape-vine trimmings; or branches of aromatic herbs such as rosemary, thyme, or sage.

For a true Texas-style barbecue, there's only one cut of meat to use: a brisket of beef. The meat is cooked very slowly over low heat to release the fat and to give time for aromatic smoke from hickory or mesquite chips to add its distinctive flavour. Serve with the traditional summer accompaniments: creamy potato salad, coleslaw, slices of ripe tomatoes, grilled country sourdough or corn bread and, of course, corn on the cob. Makes great sandwiches, too!

1. Combine oil, lemon, garlic, and seasonings. Rub all over beef and seal in a plastic bag, or set in a shallow dish to marinate in the refrigerator 6 hours or overnight.

2. Build a charcoal fire and allow the coals to burn down, or preheat gas grill to medium-low heat, adding aromatic wood chips if you like. Bring meat to room temperature, remove from marinade, and place on grill over a drip pan, fat side up.

3. Cook using low (220°F–250°F/110°C–120°C), indirect heat (see p. 63), until meat is tender and cooked through (4–5 hours); add more wood chips every now and again. Turn occasionally and brush with marinating mixture. When done, the beef should have an internal temperature of 150°F (65°C).

4. Brush with barbecue sauce during last 15 minutes of cooking. Serve hot, cut in slices across the grain, with bowls of warm barbecue sauce on the side.

Serves 6.

Tangy Texas Barbecue Sauce

1 tbsp	olive oil	15 ml
1	**medium onion,** *finely chopped*	
2 cloves	**garlic,** *finely chopped*	
2	**jalapeño peppers,** *seeded and finely chopped*	
½ cup	cider vinegar	125 ml
½ cup	dark brown sugar	125 ml
½ cup	beef bouillon	125 ml
2 cups	tomato sauce	500 ml
¼ cup	Worcestershire sauce	60 ml
1 tsp	dry mustard	5 ml
½ tsp	allspice	2 ml
	salt and freshly ground pepper	

Equally good on smoky barbecued brisket or a basic burger. For a spicier sauce, try the variation below.

1. Heat oil in a heavy saucepan over medium heat, add onion, garlic, and jalapeños, and cook until softened.

2. Stir in vinegar, brown sugar, and bouillon and cook down, stirring occasionally, until mixture is quite syrupy.

3. Stir in remaining ingredients and simmer for 15 minutes.

4. Adjust seasoning. For a smooth basting and dipping sauce, press the mixture through a sieve.

Makes 2 cups (500 ml).

TIP:

• For a spicier sauce, melt 1 tbsp (15 ml) butter in a small frying pan over medium heat. Stir in ¼ tsp (1 ml) each ground cloves, cinnamon, and allspice, and a pinch of nutmeg. Stir over heat for 1 minute, then add mixture to barbecue sauce. Simmer for a few minutes for flavours to blend.

Basic Herb Marinade

½ cup	olive oil	125 ml
¼ cup	fresh lemon juice	60 ml
	freshly ground pepper	
1 tbsp	fresh herbs, *chopped,* or	15 ml
1 tsp	dried herbs *(see Tips, below)*	5 ml
1	shallot *or* green onion, *chopped (optional)*	
1 clove	garlic, *minced (optional)*	

This simple marinade can be used with meats, poultry, fish, seafood, or vegetables. It makes an excellent base to which you can add your own favourite herbs. If you're cooking meat or fish with a high natural fat content, simply reduce the amount of oil in the marinade so the ratio of oil to acid is 1 to 1.

1. Combine ingredients thoroughly with a whisk.

Makes ¾ cup (175 ml).

TIPS:

• For the herbs in this marinade, try tarragon or thyme, especially fresh lemon thyme, when marinating chicken, veal, fish, steak, or vegetables.

• With lamb, use mint, rosemary, or oregano.

• For fish, shellfish, and vegetables, add tarragon, fresh dill, or parsley.

• To make an excellent marinade for swordfish, replace half the lemon juice in the basic marinade with balsamic vinegar, and add chopped fresh Italian parsley.

• For steak or lamb, replace half the lemon juice with red wine or balsamic vinegar, and add a sliced onion, minced garlic, cracked peppercorns, and rosemary or thyme.

• Try a good-quality balsamic vinegar on its own as a marinade for steak.

• Replace lemon juice with lime juice and use chopped fresh coriander in a marinade for swordfish, tuna, chicken, pork, trout, or vegetables.

Marinades are a combination of an acidic element (like vinegar or citrus juice), an oil, and flavourings. For a basic marinade, 2 parts oil to 1 part acid works well.

Steak Fajitas

3 lbs	flank steak	1.5 kg
2 tbsp	olive oil	30 ml
¼ cup	fresh lime juice	60 ml
½–1 tbsp	chile powder	8–15 ml
1 tsp	ground cumin	5 ml
1 tsp	garlic, *finely minced*	5 ml

TIPS:

•The basic fajita toppings are guacamole (p. 25), pico de gallo (a tomato relish, p. 111), and salsa (p. 41). (Have several types on hand, with different degrees of heat.) You can also put out bowls of chopped jalapeño peppers, sour cream, chopped onions, and grated mild Cheddar or Monterey Jack cheese.

• Plan on two 8"–10" (20–25 cm) tortillas per person, but have an extra package or two on hand, just in case. Warm tortillas before serving: Either wrap a stack in a tea towel and set on a rack over a large pot of boiling water for a couple of minutes, or wrap in foil and warm in a 325°F (160°C) oven for 10 minutes. At serving time, keep tortillas wrapped in foil or a warm towel.

Fajitas – thin slices of grilled meat rolled in tortillas with a variety of toppings – make a great informal and easy dinner for a crowd. Set out the platter of sliced meat accompanied by warm tortillas and bowls of toppings, and let guests assemble their own meal. Serve with a salad (the Corn & Black Bean Salsa, p. 110, complements the flavour of the fajitas nicely) and cold beer or a pitcher of sangría. Thinly sliced Chile-Rub Chicken (p. 63) also makes an excellent filling for fajitas.

1. Combine oil, lime juice, and seasonings, and rub well into steak on all sides. Leave to marinate in the refrigerator in a covered container or sealed plastic bag for several hours or overnight.

2. About half an hour before meal time, remove meat from the refrigerator. Prepare a charcoal fire or preheat a gas barbecue. Grill steak 5 minutes, then turn and grill 3–5 minutes more, until steak is cooked as you like it.

3. Remove to a warm platter and let rest for 5 minutes to allow the juices to be absorbed back into the meat. With a sharp knife, cut thin slices at a 45° angle across the grain and serve with tortillas and toppings.

Serves 6–8.

The trick to easy-to-handle fajitas: Fold one end of the tortilla over the filling, fold in the two sides, and then roll up. And don't put too much filling inside!

Oriental Steak

2 lbs	steak,	1 kg
	1"–1½" (2–3 cm) thick (blade, cross rib, sirloin tip, inside round)	

Oriental Marinade

¼ cup	soy sauce	60 ml
2 tbsp	lemon juice	30 ml
1 tbsp	brown sugar	15 ml
2 cloves	garlic, *finely chopped*	
1 tbsp	fresh ginger, *grated*	15 ml
2 tbsp	green onion, *chopped*	30 ml
2 tbsp	sesame oil	30 ml
½ tsp	hot sauce	2 ml
pinch	freshly ground black pepper	

TIP:

• When you're doing supper on the barbecue, grill an extra piece of steak (or chicken or pork) to use in a salad the following day. This recipe, for instance, is excellent in Oriental Beef Salad (p. 94).

This steak makes an amazing sandwich served hot or cold on a fresh crusty bun with mustard and crisp lettuce. Of course, it also makes a fabulous dinner, served with grilled peppers (p. 91), corn, and a baked potato with all the trimmings. You can use less-tender (and less-expensive) cuts with this recipe, as the marinade tenderizes along with providing wonderful flavour.

1. Trim excess fat from meat and pierce all over with a fork. Place in a covered dish or heavy-duty plastic bag, and pour in Oriental Marinade. Marinate for several hours or overnight in the refrigerator.

2. Bring meat to room temperature, remove from marinade, and cook directly over moderate heat. Grill for 6–8 minutes, brush with marinade, turn, and continue cooking until desired doneness.

3. Remove steak and let it rest for a couple of minutes to allow the juices to retreat back into the meat. Then cut into thin slices across the grain.

Serves 4.

Oriental Marinade

1. Combine all ingredients. Store in a covered jar in the refrigerator.

Makes ½ cup (125 ml).

ALSO GREAT WITH:

• Marinate small cubes of pork using the Oriental Marinade and make pork kebabs.

• Terrific with fish. See recipe, p. 83.

Mexicali Ribs

6 lbs	meaty pork back ribs	3 kg
½ cup	Mexicali Spice Rub *(recipe on p.62)*	125 ml
	Rib Baste	

Rib Baste

¼ cup	apple cider vinegar	60 ml
¼ cup	lemon juice	60 ml
¼ cup	liquid honey	60 ml
2 tbsp	olive oil	30 ml
1 tbsp	hot sauce	15 ml

This recipe calls for a long, slow baking of the ribs in a low oven, then a quick finish on the barbecue – and the results are fantastic. (Our tasters rated them the best ribs they ever had.) The oven baking can be done earlier in the day, or even the day before.

1. Cut racks of ribs in half or keep whole if your pan is big enough; wipe dry and rub all over with Mexicali Spice Rub.

2. Set in a single layer in roasting pan(s) and slow-roast in a 200°F (80°C) oven for about 3 hours. Set aside or refrigerate until needed.

3. Return to room temperature. Place ribs on a clean, lightly oiled grill over medium-high heat and sear for a few minutes on each side. Baste with Rib Baste and close the lid of the barbecue.

4. Turn and baste several times for about 30 minutes until ribs are tender and nicely charred, but still deliciously saucy.

Serves 6.

Rib Baste

1. Combine ingredients in a small saucepan. Stir over low heat until the honey melts.

Makes about 1 cup (250 ml).

Overleaf: Teriyaki Salmon (p. 80), Mexicali Ribs (this page), and grilled corn (p. 90).

Honey-Garlic Wings

24	chicken wings	
	Honey-Garlic Marinade	
½ cup	sesame seeds	125 ml

Honey-Garlic Marinade

3 tbsp	oil	45 ml
3 tbsp	liquid honey	45 ml
1 tbsp	lemon juice *or* **wine vinegar**	15 ml
½ cup	soy sauce	125 ml
1 tbsp	fresh ginger, *grated*	15 ml
2 tsp	garlic, *finely minced*	10 ml
2	green onions, *finely chopped*	

TIP:
• There are approximately 5 wings – or 10 wing pieces – to the pound (500 g).

If you like a dipping sauce, make up an extra recipe of the marinade. Simmer for 5 minutes, strain, and serve alongside the wings.

1. Cut off and discard tips from wings, and cut wings in two at the joint. Coat well in marinade and refrigerate for several hours.

2. Remove wings from marinade and barbecue over medium heat for 10 minutes. Turn wings over, baste with marinade, and sprinkle with half the sesame seeds; cook 10 minutes more. Turn, baste, sprinkle the other side with sesame seeds, and continue to cook until crisp and golden, about 10–15 minutes longer.

Makes 48 pieces.

Honey-Garlic Marinade

1. Combine ingredients well.

Makes about 1 cup (250 ml).

TIPS:
• These wings can also be done in the oven: Set them on a grill rack over a baking sheet in a 350°F (180°C) oven and proceed as above, increasing the cooking time to about 45 minutes.

• You can cook the wings ahead of time and refrigerate them until ready to serve. Then brush wings with a little fresh marinade and put them under the broiler or back on the grill for about 5 minutes to glaze and reheat them.

Smokin' Wings *with Chipotle Marinade*

24	**chicken wings**	
	Chipotle Marinade	
	guacamole *(recipe on p. 25)*	
	sour cream	

Chipotle Marinade

2	**chipotle peppers in adobo**, *finely chopped*	
3 cloves	**garlic**, *finely chopped*	
¼ cup	**olive oil**	60 ml
¼ cup	**lime juice**	60 ml
¼ cup	**soy sauce**	60 ml
1 tsp	**oregano**	5 ml
1 tsp	**basil**	5 ml

TIPS:

•The wings can also be cooked in the oven at 350°F (180°C) for about 45 minutes.

•The marinade will keep at least a week in the fridge.

• Try adding a chipotle or two to other barbecue sauces and marinades; these smoked jalapeño peppers add a distinctive, delicious flavour.

The spicy, smoky taste of the Chipotle Marinade is also delicious on chicken pieces, pork kebabs, and fajitas. Roasted chipotle peppers in adobo sauce – a type of tomato sauce – are available in cans in the Mexican section of some supermarkets and specialty food stores.

1. Cut off and discard tips from wings, and cut wings in two at the joint. Toss with marinade and refrigerate for an hour or two.

2. Remove wings from marinade and barbecue over medium heat, turning frequently until wings are evenly browned and cooked through, about 30–45 minutes.

3. Boil remaining marinade for about 5 minutes (to kill off any bacteria from the raw chicken). Brush wings with marinade during last 15 minutes of cooking time. Serve wings with guacamole and sour cream for dipping.

Makes 48 pieces.

Chipotle Marinade

1. Mix all ingredients together in a stainless-steel or glass bowl and set aside, covered, in the refrigerator until needed.

Makes ¾ cup (175 ml).

Thai-Style Wings

24	chicken wings	
2 tbsp	garlic, *chopped*	30 ml
1 tsp	ground coriander	5 ml
1 tsp	turmeric	5 ml
3–4	small, dried red chile peppers, *soaked, seeded, and chopped*	
1 tsp	curry powder	5 ml
1 tbsp	sugar	15 ml
pinch	salt	
	grated rind of 1 lemon	
3 tbsp	fish sauce *or* soy sauce	45 ml
¼ cup	coconut milk	60 ml
	Spicy Dipping Sauce (recipe on facing page)	

This version of North America's favourite bar snack requires some organization of ingredients – but nothing too exotic. Fish sauce (nam pla) is available in Asian markets, but if you can't find it, substitute a good soy sauce, preferably one of the new light sauces.

1. Trim tips from chicken wings and discard. Cut each wing in two at the joint.

2. Mash together garlic, spices, sugar, salt, and lemon rind, or whirl together in a food processor to make a paste. Stir in fish sauce or soy sauce. Coat chicken wings thoroughly in mixture. Cover and marinate overnight in the refrigerator.

3. Brush wings with coconut milk, and barbecue over medium heat, turning frequently until wings are evenly browned and cooked through, about 30–45 minutes. Serve hot or cool with Spicy Dipping Sauce.

Makes 48 pieces.

TIP:

•Cans of coconut milk are sold in many supermarkets. (Don't confuse it with cream of coconut, which is used in piña coladas.) Or you can make your own: Thoroughly mix ½ cup (125 ml) unsweetened grated dried coconut with ¾ cup (175 ml) hot water. Leave to soak for 15 minutes, then strain, squeezing the coconut pulp to extract all the liquid. Yields about ½ cup (125 ml).

Thai-Style Wings are a great choice when you want something a little more substantial at happy hour. Serve with Spicy Dipping Sauce and plenty of napkins.

Spicy Dipping Sauce

1	**small, dried red chile,** *soaked, seeded, and chopped*	
¼ cup	**fish sauce** *or* **light soy sauce** *(or part soy/part stock, to reduce saltiness)*	60 ml
1 tbsp	**brown sugar**	15 ml
2 tbsp	**lemon juice**	30 ml
1 tsp	**garlic,** *finely chopped*	
pinch	**salt** *(omit if using soy sauce)*	
1	**green onion,** *chopped*	
1 tbsp	**fresh coriander,** *chopped*	15 ml
1 tbsp	**fresh ginger,** *grated (optional)*	15 ml

Also try this dipping sauce with chicken and pork satays and grilled shrimp.

1. Combine all ingredients except green onion, coriander, and ginger. Heat until sugar dissolves.

2. Set aside to cool, then add remaining ingredients.

Makes a scant ½ cup (100 ml).

Chicken Satay
with Cheaters' Peanut Sauce

4	**chicken breasts,** *skinned and boned*	
	Lime & Coriander Marinade *(recipe on p. 82)*	
	Cheaters' Peanut Sauce	

Cheaters' Peanut Sauce

½ cup	**crunchy peanut butter**	**125 ml**
2 tbsp	**soy sauce**	**30 ml**
1 tbsp	**lemon juice**	**15 ml**
1 tbsp	**rice vinegar**	**15 ml**
1 tsp	**fresh ginger,** *minced*	**5 ml**
1 tsp	**garlic,** *minced*	**5 ml**
dash	**chile flakes** *or* **hot sauce**	
1 tbsp	**fresh coriander** *or* **parsley,** *chopped*	**15 ml**
½ cup	**warm water** *(approx.)*	**125 ml**

ALSO GREAT WITH:

•The satays can also be made with strips of pork, shrimp, or scallops.

Satays – small pieces of meat threaded on bamboo skewers and grilled – are extremely popular in Indonesia, Thailand, and Malaysia. They're great for cocktail-hour snacks, or supper, or even to take along on a picnic and cook over a campfire. Serve for dinner with a couple of salads: Napa Cabbage Salad (p. 118) and Brown Rice Salad (p. 120) would go well.

1. Pound chicken breasts lightly to flatten, and cut into narrow slices. Cover with Lime & Coriander Marinade and refrigerate, covered, for at least several hours or overnight.

2. Soak bamboo skewers in cold water for 15 minutes. Thread chicken strips on the skewers and grill, basting with a little oil and turning frequently, until nicely browned and cooked through – about 10 minutes. Serve hot with Cheaters' Peanut Sauce or Spicy Dipping Sauce (p. 57).

Serves 4–6.

Cheaters' Peanut Sauce

Genuine Indonesian peanut sauce starts with whole peanuts; this version cheats by using peanut butter. Add chopped roasted peanuts before serving if you like.

1. Combine all ingredients except the water in a food processor using on/off pulses, or mix well with a fork. Add warm water to thin as necessary. Warm sauce gently before serving.

Makes about 1 cup (250 ml).

Rotisserie-Roasted Chicken

2	whole chickens	
	(2¹⁄₂ –3 lbs/ 1–1.5 kg each)	
1 tsp	each paprika, cumin, chile powder, and freshly ground pepper	5 ml
¹⁄₂ tsp	salt	2 ml
2 tbsp	oil	30 ml
	Tangy Texas Barbecue Sauce (recipe on p.45), or your own favourite	

TIP:

• To truss a chicken, you need a long piece of strong, cotton butcher's twine. Place the chicken on its back with the string centred under the tail. Bring each end of string up and around the opposite drumstick. Pull the ends of string to bring the legs and tail close together. Turn the bird on its breast. Bring one end of string under the thigh, then repeat with the other end. Draw both ends forward and around the opposite wing, tucking in the tip. Turn the chicken, snug up the string, and tie the ends across the breast, making sure the wings are secured.

It's well worth getting a rotisserie for your barbecue – if only to roast chickens. The meat is moist, succulent, and flavourful. If you want fabulously crispy skin, just skip the brushing with barbecue sauce at the end. It's a good idea to roast two birds at a time; this chicken is so good you will definitely want to have leftovers.

1. Rinse chickens in cold water and pat dry inside and out. Remove any excess fat. Season the cavities with salt and pepper. Truss the birds to make a compact shape and keep the wings and legs from flopping as the spit turns. (See Tip, below.) Combine the spices, salt, and oil, and rub the mixture all over the chickens. Set aside for 15 minutes or so at room temperature.

2. Arrange the birds on the spit, and secure with pronged rotisserie forks, two for each bird. If you wish, place a drip pan underneath to reduce flare-ups. Roast in a covered grill for 1¹⁄₄ hours at 400˚F (200˚C), or until the chicken juices run clear and the internal temperature registers 180˚F (82˚C).

3. Since the chickens baste themselves as they turn, you only need to give them an occasional brush with some of the pan juices, or beer, and then barbecue sauce during the last 15 minutes of cooking. Let the chickens rest 15 minutes before carving.

Serves 4–6.

Chicken Tikka

4	chicken breasts, *boned and skinned*	
1	large onion, *finely chopped*	
4 cloves	garlic, *minced*	
1 piece	fresh ginger, *minced* (1"/2.5 cm)	
	juice of 1 lemon	
1 tbsp	curry powder	15 ml
¼ tsp	cinnamon	1 ml
¼ tsp	cumin	1 ml
pinch	cayenne	
	salt and freshly ground pepper	
¼ cup	oil	60 ml
1 cup	yoghurt	250 ml
	oil *or* clarified butter *(for basting)*	

If it looks like happy hour may turn into supper, consider marinating small pieces of chicken, threading them on bamboo skewers, and grilling them on the barbecue. This fragrant Indian marinade gives the chicken a lovely colour and taste. Serve the skewered chicken with a fruit chutney dip, either straight from the grill or at room temperature. The pieces can also be wrapped in warm tortillas or tucked into pita breads with shredded iceberg lettuce and chutney on top.

1. Blend onion, garlic, ginger, lemon juice, and spices to form a paste. (A blender does the job in a second, or you can use muscle power and a mortar and pestle or a bowl and a fork.) Add oil and yoghurt. Set aside.

2. Pound chicken breasts to flatten and cut into long narrow slices. Coat chicken in the marinade and leave for several hours in the refrigerator.

3. Soak bamboo skewers in water for 15 minutes. Thread the marinated chicken strips on the skewers and grill, turning and basting with a little oil or clarified butter, for about 10 minutes or until nicely browned and cooked through.

Serves 4–6.

ALSO GREAT WITH:

• This recipe also works well with small strips of beef or cubes of pork or lamb.

Add a Brown Rice Salad (p. 120) and spicy or plain grilled corn (p. 90), and turn the Chicken Tikka appetizers into dinner.

Two Spice Rubs for Grilling

Spicy Chile Rub

2 tsp	each ground cumin, coriander, and sweet paprika	10 ml
½ tsp	cinnamon	2 ml
¼ tsp	cayenne	1 ml
1 tsp	salt	5 ml
2 tbsp	fresh lime juice	30 ml
3 tbsp	olive oil	45 ml
4 cloves	garlic, *minced*	
1	jalapeño pepper, *seeded and finely chopped*	
1 tsp	fresh ginger, *grated (optional)*	5 ml

Mexicali Spice Rub

2 tbsp	cumin, *ground*	30 ml
2 tbsp	freshly ground black pepper	30 ml
2 tbsp	chile powder	30 ml
4 tbsp	paprika	60 ml
2 tbsp	oregano	30 ml
2 tbsp	sugar	30 ml
1 tbsp	salt	15 ml
2 tsp	cayenne	10 ml

Spice rubs are concentrated mixes of herbs and spices that are rubbbed all over the surface of the meat before grilling. There are dry rubs (like the Mexicali Spice Rub), and wet, more paste-like ones (like the Spicy Chile Rub).

Spicy Chile Rub

This spice rub adds flavour to chicken (use it for Chile-Rub Chicken, facing page) and is also excellent on pork. It will keep in a covered jar in the refrigerator for about a week.

1. Combine all the ingredients in a small bowl. Store in the refrigerator, tightly covered, until ready to use.

Makes ½ cup (125 ml).

Mexicali Spice Rub

Make double the quantity and store this multi-purpose mixture in a jar. Rub it on ribs (Mexicali Ribs, p. 51), chicken, or pork chops before grilling, or try it as a general seasoning sprinkled on fried potatoes, rice, or even cauliflower. You can make it as fiery as you like by adding more cayenne or chile powder.

1. Combine all ingredients and mix thoroughly.

Makes almost 1 cup (235 ml).

Chile-Rub Chicken

3 lbs	chicken pieces	1.5 kg
½ cup	Spicy Chile Rub	125 ml
	(recipe on facing page)	

The grilled chicken can be removed from the bone, sliced thinly, and used to make fajitas. (See p. 48.) Or you can serve the chicken on the bone, accompanied by a plate of grilled vegetables (p. 90) and Garlic Roast Potatoes (p. 122).

1. Rub the Spicy Chile Rub all over the chicken pieces. Place in a plastic bag and close securely, or in a covered container, and set in the refrigerator for several hours or overnight.

2. About an hour before serving, remove chicken from refrigerator and preheat the barbecue. Grill chicken with the lid closed using medium, indirect heat for about 30 minutes or until chicken is done. Remove to a warm platter and let rest for 5 minutes. If serving in tortillas, remove meat from the bone and cut in slices.

Serves 6.

BARBECUING TIPS:

• Watch the heat. If your barbecue does not have an accurate temperature gauge – few of them are – place an oven thermometer inside on the rack over the unlit burner.

• Set a timer for the approximate cooking time. It's all too easy to become distracted – especially when you have guests – and end up with dinner done to a crisp.

BARBECUING TIPS:

• When cooking larger cuts of meat or bone-in chicken on the grill without a rotisserie, use the indirect-heat method:

With a gas barbecue:

— Place a foil pan under the rack that will hold the meat.

— Preheat the grill.

— Turn off one burner after the preheating and position the meat over the unlit burner. The heat from the lit burner on the other side then circulates throughout the barbecue, cooking the meat without a direct flame under it, so your dinner doesn't turn out charred on the outside and raw on the inside. (On 3-burner grills, the centre burner is usually turned off and the meat positioned over it.)

With a covered charcoal grill:

— Place a foil pan in the bottom and bank the coals on either side of it. Put the meat on the rack over the pan, and set the cover in place.

Caribbean Chicken Parcels

4	**chicken breasts,** *boned and skinned*	
2–3 tbsp	**olive oil**	**30–45 ml**
1 tbsp	**lemon juice**	**15 ml**
	salt and freshly ground pepper	
	Ginger-Lime Butter	
2	**large carrots,** *cut into thin strips*	
2	**stalks celery,** *cut into thin strips*	
1/2 cup	**fresh coriander,** *chopped*	**125 ml**
2	**green onions,** *chopped*	

Ginger-Lime Butter

1/2 cup	**unsalted butter,** *softened*	**125 ml**
1 tbsp	**fresh ginger,** *grated*	**15 ml**
1–2 cloves	**garlic,** *finely chopped*	
	zest of 1 lime, *grated*	
1 tbsp	**lime juice**	**15 ml**
pinch	**red pepper flakes** *(optional)*	
	salt and freshly ground pepper	

The chicken and vegetables are prepared beforehand, wrapped in foil, refrigerated, and then cooked at the last minute. Each person gets his or her own parcel.

1. Sprinkle the boneless chicken breasts with a little olive oil, lemon juice, and salt and pepper, and set aside to marinate 30 minutes at room temperature, or longer in the refrigerator.

2. Heat 1 tbsp (15 ml) olive oil in a large frying pan. Lightly brown the chicken breasts – a couple of minutes per side.

3. Cut 4 large squares of heavy-duty foil. Spread each square with about 1/2 tbsp (7 ml) Ginger-Lime Butter and place a mound of carrots and celery and a chicken breast on top. Sprinkle with the coriander and green onions, season to taste, and top with another 1/2 tbsp (7 ml) Ginger-Lime Butter. Close foil to make 4 secure packages. Refrigerate parcels until needed.

4. Cook parcels over a hot fire for 20–25 minutes, turning once. Open a package after about 15 minutes to check for doneness.

Serves 4.

Ginger-Lime Butter

1. Mash all ingredients together and set aside, covered, in the refrigerator.

Makes a generous 1/2 cup (125 ml).

TIP:
• The parcels can also be cooked in a 375°F (190°C) oven, or taken on a picnic and cooked over a campfire.

Jerked Chicken or Pork

3–4 lbs	pork loin	1.5–2 kg
	or	
6	chicken breasts,	
	bone in (about 3 lbs/1.5 kg)	
	Jerk Marinade	

Jerk Marinade

1 tsp	each black pepper, thyme, cayenne, allspice, brown sugar, and salt	5 ml
½ tsp	each nutmeg and cinnamon	2 ml
¼ cup	vegetable oil	60 ml
¼ cup	orange juice	60 ml
2 tbsp	lime juice	30 ml
2 tbsp	soy sauce	30 ml
1	small onion, finely chopped	
4 cloves	garlic, finely chopped	
1	small hot chile, seeded and chopped	

"Jerk" refers to a favourite cooking method in the Caribbean. Traditionally, chicken, pork, goat, or fish is rubbed with a variety of spices, and either wrapped in leaves and pit-cooked, or slow-grilled over a green-wood fire. This recipe is a simpler way to achieve the same results. Don't be deterred by the long list of spices – you'll find most of them lurking in the cupboard. Jerked food is delicious served with steamed rice, black beans, grilled sweet potatoes (p. 87), and corn.

1. Rub the meat with the Jerk Marinade, place it in a plastic bag or in a shallow dish, and refrigerate 6 hours or overnight.

2. Bring meat to room temperature while you prepare the barbecue.

3. Using a drip pan, grill pork loin over indirect medium-low heat (see Barbecuing Tip, p. 63) until it is cooked through – about 1½ hours. Pork should reach an internal temperature of 160°F (70°C). Or grill chicken breasts for about 30–45 minutes over indirect heat. Chicken should reach an internal temperature of 180°F (82°C). Baste periodically with the marinade.

Serves 6.

Jerk Marinade

1. Combine all ingredients (by hand or using a blender or food processor) to make a paste.

Makes about 1 cup (250 ml), or enough to jerk 3–4 lbs of meat.

Herb-Crusted Lamb Spare Ribs

4 lbs	lamb spare ribs	2 kg
2 cloves	garlic, *finely chopped*	
2 tbsp	dried rosemary	30 ml
2 tbsp	dried oregano	30 ml
1 tbsp	lemon rind, *finely grated*	15 ml
½ tsp	salt	2 ml
1 tbsp	freshly ground black pepper	15 ml

Less meaty than loin chops, but absolutely delicious when cooked on the grill, these lamb spare ribs go well with other foods with a Mediterranean flavour, such as grilled pita breads and a Tomato & Feta Salad (p.116). Try to get the spare ribs in a rack; trim it of visible fat and then slice into individual portions.

1. Trim excess fat from the spare ribs and wipe dry with paper towel.

2. Mash the remaining ingredients together and rub the paste evenly all over the ribs. Set aside for 1 hour at room temperature or several hours in the refrigerator to allow flavours to penetrate.

3. Barbecue ribs over low-to-moderate heat with the lid closed, turning now and again until ribs are nicely browned on all sides, about 30 minutes.

Serves 4.

Lamb spare ribs are an underused (and thus inexpensive) cut. They are excellent on the barbecue, particularly when coated with an herb crust and grilled slowly.

Wine-Marinated Lamb Chops

8–12	lamb loin chops
	(at least 1"/2.5 cm thick)
	Red Wine Marinade
	salt and freshly ground pepper
	fresh parsley, *chopped*

Red Wine Marinade

1½ cups	dry red wine	375 ml
¼ cup	red wine vinegar	60 ml
½ cup	olive oil	125 ml
2 cloves	**garlic,** *finely chopped*	
1	**bay leaf,** *torn in pieces*	
1 tbsp	**fresh rosemary,** *chopped,* **or**	15 ml
1 tsp	dried rosemary	5 ml
	freshly ground pepper	
1	**small onion,** *sliced*	

With a rich herb and smoke flavour, these grilled lamb loin chops, lightly charred on the surface, tender and juicy inside, taste unbelievably good.

1. Pat chops dry, place in a single layer in a large, shallow pan, and add marinade. Set aside for 1 hour at room temperature or several hours (even overnight) in the refrigerator, turning meat occasionally.

2. Lift meat from marinade, pat dry, and grill over a medium-hot fire. Reserve ¼ cup (60 ml) of the marinade for basting the meat and strain the remainder into a small saucepan. Grill chops 6–8 minutes a side for medium-rare, basting with reserved marinade.

3. Simmer remaining marinade until reduced by about half, and season to taste. Serve over chops and garnish with parsley.

Serves 4–6.

Red Wine Marinade

1. Combine all ingredients thoroughly.

Makes about 2½ cups (625 ml).

ALSO GREAT WITH:

• This gutsy marinade is excellent for tenderizing and flavouring large cuts of lamb or beef, as well as steaks and kebabs.

• Try it with a butterflied leg of lamb, marinating the lamb for several hours at room temperature or overnight in the fridge. Grill the lamb following the directions in the Tip on p. 69, then slice and serve, brushing with the reduced marinade as above.

Marinated Stuffed Leg of Lamb
with Mint-Yoghurt Sauce

3½–4 lbs	boned leg of lamb	1.5–2 kg
2 cloves	garlic, *finely chopped*	
1 tsp	salt	5 ml
½ tsp	freshly ground pepper	2 ml
1 tsp	each dried thyme and oregano	5 ml
1	bay leaf	
¼ cup	lemon juice	60 ml
¼ cup	olive oil	60 ml
	Savoury Meat Stuffing *(recipe on p. 71)*	
	Mint-Yoghurt Sauce *(recipe on p. 71)*	

TIP:

• For a simple preparation, barbecue the butterflied lamb leg without the stuffing. Marinate the lamb overnight as above. Remove the meat from the marinade and set flat on a preheated grill over medium-high indirect heat, with a pan underneath to catch the drippings. Grill 15–20 minutes per side for medium-rare; allow to rest 10 minutes before carving. Serve in thin slices cut across the grain.

Lamb steeped in an herb-flavoured marinade and cooked on the barbecue is a personal favourite. You can often find a boned leg of lamb in the freezer section of the supermarket, or you can ask your butcher to bone and butterfly a whole, fresh leg for you.

1. Butterfly the boned leg of lamb: Spread it out flat, trim away excess fat or sinew, and pound lightly to flatten, slashing the thicker sections to make the piece as flat as possible.

2. Rub on all sides with garlic, salt, and pepper. Combine spices, lemon juice, and olive oil, and pour over the meat; marinate overnight in the refrigerator. At the same time, prepare the Savoury Meat Stuffing.

3. The next day, remove the lamb from the marinade, spread it out flat, and pat the stuffing in an even layer over the cut side (the side that was nearest the bone). Roll up the meat, jelly-roll style, to enclose the stuffing, and tie securely several times along the length to make a compact shape.

4. Preheat barbecue, then set meat on the rack over a drip pan; close cover and roast, using indirect, moderate heat. Remove the meat when the internal temperature registers just below 140°F (60°C) for rare; 160°F (70°C) for medium (about 22–25 minutes per pound). Set meat aside to rest for 10 minutes before slicing.

Serves 6.

(The Marinated Stuffed Leg of Lamb is shown on the next page.)

Savoury Meat Stuffing

½ cup	onion *finely chopped*	125 ml
1 tbsp	olive oil	15 ml
2 slices	good-quality white bread, *crusts removed*	
1 lb	ground beef, *or* use half beef, half lamb	500 g
1 tsp	dried oregano	5 ml
1 tbsp	each fresh mint and parsley *chopped*	15 ml
1 clove	garlic, *finely chopped*	
1 tsp	lemon zest, *grated*	5 ml
1	egg, *beaten*	
½ tsp	each salt and freshly ground pepper	2 ml

Mint-Yoghurt Sauce

1 cup	plain yoghurt	250 ml
1 tsp	lemon juice	5 ml
1 tsp	olive oil	5 ml
1 tbsp	mint, *finely chopped*	15 ml
	salt and freshly ground pepper	

Savoury Meat Stuffing

1. Cook onion in oil until soft. Soak bread briefly in a little milk or water, then squeeze dry.

2. Combine all ingredients and blend together well. Refrigerate until needed.

Makes about 3 cups (750 ml).

TIP:

• Also try the stuffing made into patties, grilled, and tucked into warm pita breads with chopped tomato, onion, cucumber, and Mint-Yoghurt Sauce on top.

Mint-Yoghurt Sauce

1. Gently combine all ingredients. Taste and adjust seasoning, and refrigerate for an hour or so before serving.

Makes 1 cup (250 ml).

BARBECUING TIPS:

•An instant-read thermometer is handy when you're barbecuing large cuts of meat. Slip the tip into the fleshiest part, and it provides a quick, accurate reading of the internal temperature. (This type of thermometer does not remain in the meat.) For beef and lamb, the internal temperature should be 140°F (60°C) for rare; 160°F (70°C) for medium, and 170°F (75°C) for well done; pork should be cooked to an internal temperature of 160°F (70°C).

• Remove meat from the barbecue when the internal temperature is about 10°F below the desired temperature; cover it with foil and allow it to rest for 10 minutes before carving.

Marinated Stuffed Leg of Lamb with Mint-Yoghurt Sauce (p. 69) and Tomato & Feta Salad (p. 116).

Indian-Style Lamb Kebabs

2 lbs	**lamb,** *boned, trimmed, and cut into 1½" (3-cm) cubes*	**1 kg**
1 tsp	**cumin**	**5 ml**
1 tsp	**garam masala** *or* **good curry powder**	**5 ml**
¼ tsp	**turmeric**	**2 ml**
½ cup	**plain yoghurt**	**125 ml**
2 tbsp	**fresh ginger,** *finely chopped*	**30 ml**
2 cloves	**garlic,** *finely chopped*	
½	**small onion,** *finely chopped*	
	salt and freshly ground pepper	

Marinated chunks of lean lamb from a boneless leg make wonderful kebabs. Serve the kebabs with basmati rice, Spicy Grilled Corn (p. 90), the cooling Indian yoghurt dip known as raita (see Quick Tricks, below), and a fruit chutney.

1. Combine all ingredients except lamb.

2. Coat lamb pieces with marinade mixture and seal in a plastic bag or set in a shallow, covered dish; refrigerate for 6 hours or overnight.

3. Bring lamb to room temperature and thread on skewers.

4. Grill over medium-high heat until kebabs are nicely browned on the outside and tender and juicy inside (8–10 minutes).

Serves 6.

QUICK TRICKS:

• Raita is the traditional yoghurt mixture served with Indian foods. Combine 1 cup (250 ml) peeled and grated cucumber with 1½ cups (375 ml) plain yoghurt, ½ tsp (2 ml) salt, 1 tbsp (15 ml) fresh chopped mint (or 1 tsp/5 ml dried), 1 tsp (5 ml) toasted cumin seeds, and a pinch of black pepper and paprika. Chill before serving.

• For variety, make a spinach raita: Prepare as above, omitting the cucumber, salt, and mint; just before serving, stir in about 1 cup (250 ml) chopped cooked spinach and salt to taste.

TIPS:

• If using bamboo skewers, remember to soak them in water for 15 minutes before using so they don't burn.

• Garam masala is a fragrant spice blend available in Indian markets. If you can't find it, substitute a good-quality curry powder.

• You can also use this marinade with a boned and butterflied leg of lamb. Marinate as above; see Tip p. 69 for grilling instructions.

Mexican Burgers

1 lb	lean ground beef	500 g
2 tbsp	onion, *finely chopped*	30 ml
1 clove	garlic, minced	
1 tsp	dried oregano	5 ml
1 tbsp	fresh coriander, *chopped*	15 ml
1 tsp	jalapeño pepper, *finely chopped, or* hot sauce, *to taste*	5 ml
	salt and freshly ground pepper	
dash	water *or* milk	
4 slices	Monterey Jack cheese *or* mild Cheddar cheese	

Serve these tasty burgers on lightly grilled sesame buns lined with leaf lettuce, and then pile on guacamole (p. 25), salsa (p. 41), and sour cream.

1. Combine meat, onion, garlic, herbs, and seasonings. Mix lightly and moisten with just enough water or milk so that the mixture can be formed into 8 thin patties.

2. Top 4 of the patties with a cheese slice. Top each with another patty and pinch the edges to seal.

3. Grill over medium heat for about 8 minutes, turning once about halfway through. Top burgers with guacamole and other condiments as desired.

Serves 4.

TIP:

• Use this recipe to make Mexican Mini-Meatballs, a great party snack: Double the recipe, cutting the cheese into ½" (1-cm) cubes. Pat about a tablespoonful of meat mixture around each cube to form small meatballs. Thread meatballs on skewers and grill until nicely browned and cooked through, about 8–10 minutes, turning frequently. Or place in a shallow roasting pan and cook in a covered grill over medium heat for about 30 minutes. Serve hot, with salsa and sour cream for dipping. Makes about 35 small meatballs.

Overleaf: Mexican Burgers, Indian-Style Lamb Kebabs, and Spicy Grilled Corn (p. 90).

Greek Burgers

1½ lbs	ground lamb *or* beef	750 g
1	small onion, *grated*	
1 clove	garlic, *minced*	
½ cup	soft breadcrumbs	125 ml
1	egg yolk	
1 tsp	ground cumin	5 ml
½ tsp	oregano	2 ml
¼ tsp	cinnamon	1 ml
	salt and freshly ground pepper	
6	pita breads	
	tzatziki and Greek salad *(optional, for topping burgers)*	

TIP:

• Use the meat mixture to make small meatballs. Thread meatballs on bamboo skewers that have been soaked in water for 15 minutes (2 meatballs per skewer). Grill approximately 6 minutes per side. Serve with tzatziki for dipping.

Tuck these burgers into pita bread pockets and top with Greek Salad (p.117) and tzatziki. (See Tip, below.)

1. Toss burger ingredients lightly together.

2. Form mixture into 6 oval patties about ¾" (2 cm) thick.

3. Set burgers on a preheated grill over high heat, close the lid, and cook 3–4 minutes on the first side. Turn and cook 3–4 minutes longer to desired degree of doneness.

4. Serve in warm pita bread pockets topped with tzatziki and some Greek Salad.

Serves 6.

TIP:

• You'll find tzatziki, a yoghurt-cucumber-garlic dip, in the dairy case of the super-market. Or make your own: Combine 1 cup (250 ml) plain yoghurt with 1 small cucumber, peeled, seeded, grated, and drained; 1–2 cloves garlic, minced; and 1 tbsp (15 ml) each of chopped fresh parsley and mint (or use 1 tsp/5 ml dried mint). Season to taste and chill for an hour to allow flavours to blend.

• For the best results, use full-fat yoghurt – low-fat versions are too watery – or allow low-fat yoghurt to drain overnight in a cheesecloth bag (or in a sieve lined with paper coffee filters).

Italian Burgers

1½ lbs	ground beef	750 g
1	sweet or hot Italian sausage, *casing removed*	
1	small onion, *grated*	
¼ cup	Parmesan cheese, *grated*	60 ml
1 tsp	oregano	5 ml
pinch	chile flakes *(optional)*	
	salt and freshly ground pepper	
6 slices	mozzarella cheese	
6	kaiser buns	
½ cup	tomato sauce, *warmed*	125 ml
	grilled *or* sautéed peppers, onions, and mushrooms, *(optional, for topping burgers)*	

These burgers make a great change from ordinary cheeseburgers. Delicious topped with grilled or sautéed hot and sweet peppers, onion slices, and white or portobello mushrooms.

1. Toss burger ingredients together lightly.

2. Form into 6 patties, ³/₄" (2 cm) thick.

3. Set burgers on a preheated grill, close the lid, and cook over high heat, 3–4 minutes on the first side; then turn and cook for 2–3 minutes longer. Top each burger with a slice of mozzarella and cook for a minute more to melt the cheese.

4. Serve each burger on a warm kaiser bun brushed on the inside with tomato sauce. Top with grilled or sautéed peppers, onions, and mushrooms to taste.

Serves 6.

TIP:

• For a make-ahead supper: Add ½ cup (125 ml) soft breadcrumbs and some chopped parsley to the meat mixture and form into meatballs. Cook in your favourite tomato sauce and serve over pasta.

Chicken or Turkey Burgers

1½ lbs	ground turkey *or* **chicken**	750 g
½ cup	green onions, *finely chopped*	125 ml
1 tsp	dried thyme	5 ml
2 tbsp	flat-leaf parsley, *finely chopped*	30 ml
1	egg yolk	
½ tsp	salt	2 ml
¼ tsp	freshly ground pepper	1 ml
	olive oil	
6	whole-wheat *or* sesame buns	
	mayonnaise and butter	
	watercress *or* lettuce, cranberry sauce, and grilled onions *(optional, for topping burgers)*	

Because everyone knows the perils of eating undercooked poultry, there's an unfortunate tendency to cook chicken and turkey burgers to death. Follow these directions for moist, succulent burgers.

1. Toss the first 7 ingredients lightly together.

2. Form into 6 patties about ½" (1 cm or so) thick. Place on a platter and refrigerate for half an hour.

3. Brush burgers lightly with olive oil and place on a preheated grill. Close lid and cook over medium-high heat for 4–5 minutes, then turn and cook 3–4 minutes longer. Test after 7 minutes – burgers are done when the meat has lost its pink colour throughout and the juices run clear. (Depending on your barbecue, burgers may take a couple of minutes longer, but don't over-cook them or they'll dry out.)

4. Lightly toast buns. Spread mayonnaise on the bottom half of each bun and add watercress or lettuce and the burger. Top with a spoonful of cranberry sauce, a grilled onion slice, and the top of the bun, lightly buttered.

Serves 6.

TIPS:

• Handle the mixture lightly, tossing the ingredients together quickly with a fork.

• Lightly oil your hands before forming the burgers, to help keep the mixture from sticking to your fingers.

• Resist the desire to pat, squeeze, or prod the burgers while they are cooking, so the good juices don't end up in the fire.

Grilled Fish Steaks
with Tomato-Caper Sauce

2½ lbs	fish steaks *or* fillets (fresh tuna, swordfish, bass, *or* lake trout)	1 kg
⅓ cup	olive oil	75 ml
2	medium onions, *thinly sliced*	
4	medium tomatoes, *peeled, seeded, and chopped*	
4–5 cloves	garlic, *minced*	
1 tsp	thyme	5 ml
1	bay leaf	
2 tbsp	fresh orange juice	30 ml
1 strip	orange peel *(2"/5 cm)*	
	salt and freshly ground pepper	
¼ cup	pitted ripe olives, *chopped*	60 ml
2 tbsp	capers	30 ml
1 tbsp	balsamic vinegar *or* lemon juice *(optional)*	15 ml
pinch	sugar *(optional)*	
	thin orange slices and fresh parsley, *chopped (for garnish)*	

The sharpness of the capers, the richness of the olives, and the hint of sweetness from the orange create the complex flavour of this delicious tomato-based sauce. The fish is very good hot, but to my taste even more enjoyable at room tempera-ture – which means you have the convenience of being able to do the preparation ahead of time. Try the sauce with grilled chicken, too.

1. In a large frying pan, cook onions in ¼ cup (60 ml) oil over medium heat until soft. Add tomatoes, garlic, ½ tsp (2 ml) of the thyme, the bay leaf, the orange juice and peel, and salt and pepper. Bring to a simmer, then lower heat, cover, and cook gently for about 10 minutes until sauce begins to thicken.

2. Stir in olives and capers. Heat through. Taste and adjust flavour with a splash of vinegar or lemon juice and/or a pinch of sugar.

3. Brush the fish lightly with the remaining olive oil and season with salt, pepper, and remaining thyme. Grill, broil, or pan-fry 5–10 minutes, depending on the thickness of the fish, turning once.

4. Serve hot, covered with the sauce and garnished with parsley and orange slices. Or allow fish to cool, break into bite-sized pieces, and fold into the sauce. Cover and refrigerate until serving. Serve at room temperature gar-nished as above.

Serves 6.

Teriyaki Salmon or Tuna

4	**salmon steaks** or **fillets,** or **tuna steaks** (about 6 oz/ 200 g each)	
¼ cup	**Teriyaki Marinade**	60 ml

Teriyaki Marinade & Basting Sauce

½ cup	**soy sauce**	125 ml
¼ cup	**dry sherry**	60 ml
¼ cup	**peanut** or **olive oil**	60 ml
¼ cup	**brown sugar**	60 ml
2 cloves	**garlic,** minced	
2	**green onions,** finely chopped	
1 tsp	**fresh ginger,** grated	5 ml

Commercial varieties of teriyaki sauce are available, but your home-made version will taste better. It will keep indefinitely in a sealed bottle in the fridge. Serve the teriyaki fish with steamed rice and simple vegetables of the season.

1. Sprinkle marinade over salmon or tuna. Leave at room temperature 15–30 minutes, turning once.

2. Set salmon or tuna on a clean, lightly oiled grill over medium-high heat (or under a preheated broiler) for about 5 minutes. Brush with marinade, turn, and grill 3–5 minutes longer, depending on the thickness of the fish. Fish is done when the flesh just flakes when tested.

Serves 4.

Teriyaki Marinade & Basting Sauce

1. Combine ingredients in a small saucepan. Set over medium heat and simmer for 5 minutes, stirring to dissolve sugar. Strain and cool before using.

Makes about 1¼ cups (300 ml).

ALSO GREAT WITH:

• Teriyaki marinade is delicious with other firm fish such as swordfish and halibut, and shellfish such as shrimp and scallops. Also try it on chicken – especially chicken wings – pork, and flank steak. (For how to prepare flank steak, use the directions with the recipe on p. 48.)

Teriyaki Marinade is excellent with fresh tuna steaks. Grill them with a careful eye, so you're sure not to overcook.

Whole Grilled Fish
with Lime & Coriander Marinade

3 lbs	whole fish *(any kind, but preferably one just caught by a family angler)*	1.5 kg
	Lime & Coriander Marinade	
	salt and freshly ground pepper	
1	**lime,** *sliced*	

Lime & Coriander Marinade

½ cup	olive oil	125 ml
¼ cup	fresh lime juice	60 ml
1 tsp	lime zest, *grated*	5 ml
	freshly ground pepper	
1 tbsp	fresh coriander *or* Italian parsley, *chopped*	15 ml
2	green onions, *chopped*	
1	small, dried hot chile pepper, *crumbled* or	
dash	hot sauce	

The fish is excellent served with Gazpacho Salad (p. 119) or Napa Cabbage Salad (p. 118) and hot corn bread (p. 199).

1. Have the angler (or the folks at the fish market) clean the fish, leaving skin, head, and tail on. Make 3 diagonal slashes just through the skin, and brush the fish inside and out with Lime & Coriander Marinade. Let sit at room temperature for 15 minutes.

2. Place on a clean, lightly oiled grill over a medium-hot fire and cook 10–15 minutes, carefully turning once. Baste frequently with marinade. Fish is cooked through when flesh just flakes when tested. Season to taste and serve garnished with lime slices.

Serves 3–4.

Lime & Coriander Marinade

1. Combine ingredients thoroughly.

Makes ¾ cup (175 ml).

ALSO GREAT WITH:
• Try this marinade on fish steaks as well as whole fish; it's particularly delicious with swordfish.

•The light, fresh flavours of this marinade also complement chicken, pork, and veal.

TIP:
• A long-handled, hinged wire fish basket (available at kitchenware and some hardware stores) makes grilling the fish simple. Be sure to oil it before using.

Fish in Foil, Oriental Style

2 lbs	**whole fish**	1 kg
½ cup	**Oriental Marinade** *(recipe on p. 50)*	125 ml

Cooked on the barbecue or in the oven, fish prepared this way is delicious either hot or cold in a salad. Try red snapper, striped bass, or trout.

1. Thoroughly clean fish and pat dry. Make two slashes in the flesh on each side. Rub Oriental Marinade into the surface and inside the cavity of the fish. Set aside for 30 minutes.

2. Wrap the fish in heavy foil to make a sealed package and place on a pre-heated grill or in a 450°F (230°C) oven. Cook approximately 30 minutes – allowing 10 minutes for each 1" (2.5 cm) of fish measured at its thickest part, plus 5 minutes for the heat to penetrate the foil. Serve at once with cooking juices.

Serves 2–3.

TIP:

• To serve chilled – perhaps accompanied by a salad with a light vinaigrette such as Brown Rice Salad (p. 120) or Lemon-Cumin Couscous Salad (p. 113) – allow fish to cool slightly. While it is still warm, carefully scrape away skin and lift the flesh from the bones. Wrap well and refrigerate until serving.

Garlic Shrimp Kebabs

16	large fresh shrimp	
	Lemon-Garlic Baste	
4	green onions	
4	cherry tomatoes	
	salt	
1	lemon, *cut in wedges*	

Lemon-Garlic Baste

1–2 cloves	garlic, *minced*	
3 tbsp	olive oil *or* melted butter	45 ml
½ tsp	thyme	2 ml
½ tsp	lemon zest, *grated*	2 ml
	freshly ground pepper	

TIP:

• If you use bamboo skewers, soak them in water for **15** minutes first so they don't burn.

These kebabs make a great hot-weather dinner served with Roasted Vegetable Couscous (p. 112) or Mediterranean Potato Salad (p. 106), and some chilled white wine. Or make smaller kebabs for something special for cocktail hour.

1. Remove shells from shrimp, leaving the tails attached if you like. Cut down the back of each shrimp to remove the black intestinal vein. Rinse deveined shrimp in cold water, dry thoroughly, and coat well with Lemon-Garlic Baste. Set aside for 15 minutes at room temperature or 30 minutes in the refrigerator.

2. Trim the green onions and cut each into 3 pieces. Assemble 4 skewers, alternating shrimp and green onion and finishing with a tomato.

3. Brush assembled kebabs with Lemon-Garlic Baste and place on a hot, oiled grill. Cook about 2–3 minutes a side. (Cooking time will depend on size of shrimp. Check after 3 minutes; the shrimp should be opaque and tender.) Serve hot, seasoned with salt and fresh lemon juice.

Serves 2.

Lemon-Garlic Baste

1. Combine ingredients and set aside for 10 minutes or so to allow flavours to blend.

Makes ¼ cup (60 ml).

ALSO GREAT WITH:

• Try the Lemon-Garlic Baste brushed on lamb chops, chicken, or fish.

Ginger-Mango Shrimp Kebabs

¼ cup	soy sauce	60 ml
¼ cup	lime juice	60 ml
¼ cup	vegetable oil	60 ml
1 tbsp	fresh ginger, *grated* or	15 ml
1 tsp	ground ginger	5 ml
2 cloves	garlic, *finely chopped*	
24	large shrimp, *shelled and deveined*	
4	green onions	
1	mango	

This recipe has the spirit of the tropics. Try it when you're looking for something special for cocktail hour, or make bigger kebabs and serve for dinner.

1. Combine soy sauce, lime juice, oil, ginger, and garlic in a stainless-steel or glass bowl.

2. Add shrimp and marinate for 30 minutes in the refrigerator.

3. Clean and trim green onions and cut each into 3 pieces. Peel mango and cut into 1" (2.5-cm) chunks.

4. Soak 12 long bamboo skewers in water for 15 minutes. Thread 2 shrimp on each skewer, then place a piece of green onion and a chunk of mango on the end.

5. Barbecue over medium heat for 3–4 minutes, turning once. Serve hot.

Serves 6 for cocktail hour.

TIPS:

• Substitute small chunks of pork loin for the shrimp; just increase the grilling time to 5–6 minutes.

• If mangoes aren't available, you can substitute chunks of red and yellow peppers.

Honey-Lime Pork Loin Roast

3½–4 lbs	boneless pork loin	1.5–2 kg
1 clove	garlic, *finely chopped*	
1 tsp	oregano	5 ml
½ tsp	each ground cumin, chile powder, black pepper, and salt	2 ml
1 tbsp	lime *or* lemon juice	15 ml
1 tbsp	oil	15 ml
	Honey-Lime Basting Sauce	

Honey-Lime Basting Sauce

¼ cup	lime *or* lemon juice	60 ml
¼ cup	honey	60 ml
½ tsp	hot red pepper flakes	2 ml
1 tbsp	Dijon mustard	15 ml

A pork roast cooked on the barbecue lends itself to many flavourful marinades and basting sauces. This version has south-of-the-border accents; it's delicious served with warm tortillas, Corn & Black Bean Salsa (p. 110) and Couscous-Stuffed Tomatoes (p. 121).

1. Make a paste with the garlic, herbs, spices, lime or lemon juice, and oil, and rub on all sides of the pork. Leave to marinate several hours or overnight in the refrigerator.

2. Combine all ingredients for Honey-Lime Basting Sauce.

3. Preheat barbecue, then place pork on the grill over a drip pan. Close cover and cook using indirect, moderate heat for 1½–2 hours, brushing occasionally during the last 20 minutes of cooking with Honey-Lime Basting Sauce.

4. Pork should be cooked to an internal temperature of 160°F (70°C); slightly pink in the centre is fine. Remove from the grill when the temperature is 5°F–10°F lower and let stand 10 minutes before slicing.

Serves 6.

BARBECUING TIPS:

•In general, apply sweet sauces and bastes only towards the end of the cooking time; otherwise, the sugars in them will burn and impart a bitter taste to the meat.

• For directions on how to barbecue using indirect heat, see p. 63.

Grilled Sweet Potatoes

4	sweet potatoes,	
	peeled	
2 tbsp	butter	30 ml
1 tbsp	brown sugar	15 ml
pinch	allspice	
pinch	salt	

Sweet potatoes are often overlooked during barbecue season, but they're wonderful done on the grill. Try them with Jerked Pork or Chicken (p. 65).

1. Cut sweet potatoes into $1/4$" (5-mm) slices and toss with the remaining ingredients.

2. Cut two pieces of heavy-duty foil, pile half the potatoes on each piece, and then seal the edges.

3. Grill over medium heat for about 15–20 minutes or until tender, flipping packages occasionally during cooking.

Serves 6.

QUICK TRICK:

An Herb Butter is a delicious make-in-advance addition to grilled vegetables, meat, or fish: Cream $1/2$ cup (125 ml) soft butter with 1 tbsp (15 ml) lemon juice. Add 2 tbsp (30 ml) minced fresh herbs (parsley, chives, basil, tarragon, or rosemary). Season with salt and pepper to taste. On a piece of waxed paper, form butter into a log, wrap, and refrigerate. Slice off pats as needed and serve on food hot from the grill.

Grilled Red Onions with Cayenne

3	medium red onions	
1–2 tbsp	olive oil	15–30 ml
	paprika	
	cayenne	
a few	thyme sprigs or	
1 tsp	dried thyme	5 ml

Dynamite on top of a juicy grilled hamburger or steak sandwich, or chopped on top of a hotdog.

1. Remove skins from onions and cut into slices about $1/2$" (1 cm) thick.

2. Brush onion slices with oil and sprinkle with paprika and a dash of cayenne. Add thyme sprigs and leave to marinate for 30 minutes.

3. Place on a hot, lightly oiled grill and cook 10–12 minutes; turn and brush with marinating juices several times until nicely browned and just tender. Serve hot.

Serves 6.

TIP:

• Splash the grilled onions with a little balsamic vinegar, sprinkle with salt and freshly ground pepper, and refrigerate in a covered jar. They'll keep for a day or two – just waiting to be served as a condiment beside the perfect grilled steak.

Grilled vegetables make a wonderful antipasto platter with salami, olives, and cheese, or a great sandwich when tucked in a pita. (See pp. 90–91.)

Grilled Vegetables

IDEAS FOR USING MIXED GRILLED VEGETABLES:

• Arrange grilled sliced vegetables on a large platter – eggplant, onion, zucchini, peppers, mushrooms – season lightly with salt and pepper, and sprinkle with balsamic or red wine vinegar. Scatter a handful of chopped fresh basil and parsley on top. Serve immediately as is, as a side dish with grilled meat, chicken, or fish. Or set aside, covered, for 1 hour at room temperature or as long as overnight in the refrigerator. Bring to room temperature before serving.

•Arrange a platter of vegetables as above, sprinkling with shaved Parmesan cheese and black olives as part of an antipasto spread with salamis and other meats.

GRILLED-VEGETABLE PIZZA:

Brush pizza crust (see p. 190) with pesto or basil-flavoured olive oil. Top with chopped grilled vegetables and grated Parmesan or crumbled goat cheese. Bake in preheated 375°F (190°C) oven for 15 minutes until crust is crisp and cheese is melted.

The slightly smoky taste that comes from grilling enhances the flavour of many vegetables. Here are some basic grilling methods, along with serving suggestions.

Corn

Carefully pull back the husks and remove the silks. Smooth the husks back into place, tie them with string at the tip and in the middle, and soak in cold water for 30 minutes to saturate the husks. Drain and set on the grill over medium-high heat for 20–30 minutes, turning often.

SPICY GRILLED CORN:

Wonderful with Indian-Style Lamb Kebabs (p. 72) or Jerked Pork or Chicken (p. 65): Melt $1/4$ cup (60 ml) butter and mix with 1 tsp (5 ml) of a good curry powder or garam masala spice mix and a pinch of cayenne. Prepare corn as above and grill over medium-high heat for about 15 minutes, turning frequently. Pull husks back from cob, bunching leaves around the stalk to form a handle. Brush the kernels with the spicy butter. Grill for a few minutes more, turning frequently until the kernels are lightly charred. Salt lightly to taste.

Eggplant

Slice globe eggplants crosswise into generous $1/4$" (5-mm) slices, sprinkle with salt, and brush with plain or garlic-flavoured olive oil. (Thin, Japanese eggplants can simply be cut in half lengthwise.) Place on an oiled rack over medium heat and cook about 8–12 minutes, turning often, until the slices are tender and nicely browned, but still hold their shape.

Garlic

Slice horizontally across the top of a whole head of garlic about $1/2$" (1 cm) down from the top, exposing the ends of each clove. Rub all over with olive

IDEAS FOR USING ROASTED PEPPERS:

• Slice and serve as a salad, tossing the pepper strips with garlic-flavoured olive oil, freshly ground black pepper, chunks of feta cheese, black olives, and chopped green onion.

• Chop and add to corn bread or corn meal muffins.

• Tuck into a sandwich with meatballs, barbecued sausages, or pork schnitzel.

• Slice into strips and toss with hot pasta and a little garlic-flavoured olive oil; sprinkle with grated Parmesan cheese.

• Slice and serve alongside scrambled eggs and Italian sausage for a special weekend brunch.

• Chop and combine with chopped tomato, onion, coriander, and lime juice, and serve as a sauce with grilled fish.

• Pack sliced or puréed peppers in small containers, add olive oil just to cover, and freeze. Use on pasta, or to flavour soups, sauces, and stews.

GRILLED-VEGETABLE LASAGNE:

This makes a great light supper, served hot with crusty bread and a tossed green salad: Simply alternate layers of tomato sauce, lasagne noodles, grilled sliced vegetables, ricotta cheese, and grated mozzarella cheese in a 9" x 13" (3-L) baking dish. Bake in a preheated 350°F (180°C) oven for 20 minutes. Sprinkle with 1/2 cup (125 ml) grated Parmesan cheese, and bake about 10 minutes more until cheese is melted and beginning to brown. Sprinkle with fresh chopped parsley and serve.

oil. Wrap in foil and cook over medium-high heat about 45 minutes until soft, turning occasionally. Squeeze out the roasted cloves.

Onions

Remove skins from red and white onions, slice 1/2" (1 cm) thick, brush with olive oil, and place on an oiled grill rack over medium-high heat. Grill for 10–12 minutes, turning several times, until tender and nicely charred.

Peppers

Place red, yellow, and green peppers on barbecue rack over high heat. Roast, turning often, until evenly blistered and charred on all sides, about 5–10 minutes. Transfer to a paper bag and leave to steam for 10 minutes. Peel away charred skin; cut in half, discard stem and seeds, and slice.

Portobello Mushrooms

Remove stems. Combine plain or garlic-flavoured olive oil with an equal amount of balsamic vinegar, and season with salt and pepper. Brush mushrooms with the mixture, and allow to sit for 20–30 minutes. Grill over medium heat for about 5 minutes per side, until the mushrooms just begin to exude their juices.

Tomatoes

Cut out the tough core at the stalk end of each tomato. Cut tomatoes in half and rub with olive oil, salt, and pepper. Set on the grill over low heat for about 10–12 minutes, turning once.

Zucchini

Slice lengthwise into 1/2" (1-cm) slices. Brush with olive oil and place on a rack over medium heat. Grill 4–6 minutes, turning often.

III. SALADS & SIDE DISHES

Salads with Meat and Fish

Just add some good bread and wine and you've got a great summer meal on a hot day:

Salads with Pasta, Legumes, and Grains

Some of these recipes can also be substantial enough to form the centrepiece of a meal:

Vegetable Salads and Salsas

Dressings

Side Dishes

CROWD PLEASERS:

FOUR SUGGESTIONS FOR SPECIAL SUMMER DINNERS

When a get-together demands a dinner that's a cut above the ordinary, fire up the barbecue and try one of these summer menus:

MENU #1

Marinated Stuffed Leg of Lamb with Mint-Yoghurt Sauce *(p. 69)*

Garlic Roast Potatoes *(p. 122)*

Tomato & Feta Salad *(p. 116)*

Warm pita breads

•

MENU #2

Honey-Lime Pork Loin Roast *(p. 86)*

Mixed Grilled Vegetables *(p. 90)*

Lemon-Cumin Couscous Salad *(p. 113)*

Warm tortillas

•

MENU #3

Teriyaki Salmon Steaks *(p. 80)*

Napa Cabbage Salad *(p. 118)*

Corn & Black Bean Salsa *(p. 110)*

Warm corn bread *(p. 199)*:

•

MENU #4

Chile-Rub Chicken *(p. 63)*

Roasted Vegetable Couscous *(p. 112)*

Mixed Greens with Basic Vinaigrette *(p. 100)*

Grilled focaccia slices *(p. 200)*

Oriental Beef Salad

¼ lb	rice noodles *or* rice vermicelli	125 g
1 lb	sirloin steak, *grilled and sliced thinly across the grain*	500 g
½ cup	Oriental Dressing *(recipe on facing page)*	125 ml
½ lb	snow peas	250 g
6	dried Chinese mushrooms	
1 tbsp	vegetable oil	15 ml
2	green onions, *chopped*	
1 tsp	lemon rind, *grated*	5 ml
	fresh coriander, *chopped (optional)*	

TIPS:

• Steps 1–4 can be done early in the day and the 3 groups of ingredients refrigerated.

• To intensify the Oriental flavour of the salad, marinate the steak briefly in Oriental Marinade (p. 50) before grilling.

The components of this salad can all be prepared early in the day, so that all you have to do at dinnertime is arrange them on a platter. In fact, time in the fridge will actually improve the flavour of this dish, giving the dressing a chance to permeate the steak, noodles, and vegetables.

1. Cook the noodles in a large quantity of boiling salted water until tender, about 3–4 minutes. Drain well and toss with a little oil.

2. Remove stems and strings from snow peas and blanch in boiling water for about 30 seconds. Drain and toss immediately into ice water to stop the cooking. Drain again.

3. Remove stems from mushrooms; discard. Cover caps with boiling water and let sit until softened (about 15 minutes). Drain, slice, and stir-fry 5 minutes in oil. Add to snow peas.

4. Toss snow pea-and-mushroom mixture, noodles, and steak separately in a spoonful or two of Oriental Dressing apiece.

5. Before serving, pile noodles on a platter and arrange steak and vegetables on top. Sprinkle with green onions, lemon rind, and coriander.

Serves 4.

Two Spicy Dressings

Oriental Dressing

¼ cup	rice vinegar	60 ml
2 tbsp	soy sauce	30 ml
1 tbsp	each safflower oil *and* sesame oil	15 ml
1 clove	garlic, *minced*	
1 tbsp	fresh ginger, *finely chopped*	15 ml
1 tbsp	sugar	15 ml
½ tsp	Chinese chili sauce or	2 ml
¼ tsp	chile flakes	1 ml
pinch	salt	

Coriander-Lime Vinaigrette

2 tbsp	lime juice	30 ml
6 tbsp	oil (½ olive oil, ½ vegetable oil)	90 ml
	salt and freshly ground black pepper	
1 clove	garlic, *minced*	
1	small hot pepper, *finely chopped (or to taste)*	
¼ cup	fresh coriander, *chopped*	60 ml

Oriental Dressing

Use this dressing with the Oriental Beef Salad (opposite page).

1. Combine all ingredients in a small jar. Shake well and set aside.

Makes ½ cup (125 ml).

TIP:

• The secret ingredient in the dressing is a dash of Chinese chili sauce, available in jars at Oriental markets. If you can't find it, you can substitute red chile flakes; pound them to a paste with the garlic, ginger, and salt.

Coriander-Lime Vinaigrette

Use this dressing with the Mexican Chicken Salad (p. 98).

1. Combine all ingredients in a small jar. Shake well and set aside.

Makes ½ cup (125 ml).

TIPS:

• If you don't have fresh limes and coriander, you can substitute lemons and parsley.

• Lemons and limes vary in flavour, acidity, and the amount of juice they provide. Always taste and adjust the amount in a recipe to your liking.

Orzo with Shrimp

½ lb	orzo	250 g
¼ cup	olive oil	60 ml
	salt and freshly ground pepper	
1 lb	large shrimp, *in the shell*	500 g
1 clove	garlic, *minced*	
2 tbsp	lemon juice *(or to taste)*	30 ml
1 tbsp	Dijon mustard	15 ml
½	red pepper, *finely chopped*	
½	green pepper, *finely chopped*	
2	green onions, *finely chopped*	
½ cup	fresh parsley, *chopped*	125 ml
¼ cup	fresh dill, *chopped*	60 ml
½ cup	mayonnaise	125 ml
¼ cup	sour cream *or* yoghurt	60 ml

TIP:

• Steps 1–3 can be done early in the day and the components refrigerated.

Orzo is a small, rice-shaped pasta that makes a light, pleasant foil for all kinds of summer flavours. This salad looks wonderful arranged on a large platter lined with crisp lettuce and decorated with lemon wedges, ripe olives, and fresh chopped herbs. To extend the dish, add steamed mussels, lightly poached scallops, or monkfish. With a plate of sliced tomatoes and good crusty bread, you've got a great summer meal.

1. Cook orzo in a large quantity of boiling salted water until just tender, about 8 minutes. Drain well, and toss while still warm with a good drizzle of olive oil and freshly ground pepper. Set aside.

2. Drop shrimp into boiling salted water; when water returns to the boil simmer 2–5 minutes, depending on size. Test after 2 minutes – the shrimp should be light orange in colour, and tender but resilient to the touch. Cool and peel.

3. Make the dressing by combining the garlic, mustard, lemon juice, remaining olive oil, salt and pepper to taste, and half the parsley and dill.

4. Coat the shrimp (and any other seafood you're including) in a spoonful or two of the dressing. Toss orzo with peppers, green onions, the rest of the herbs, and enough dressing to coat and flavour the pasta. Fold in the shrimp, mayonnaise, and sour cream. The salad can be served immediately, but is even better if refrigerated for an hour or so to allow the flavours to blend.

Serves 4.

Add steamed mussels and poached monkfish to Orzo with Shrimp for a gala presentation.

Mexican Chicken Salad

4	**chicken breasts,** *bone in*	
1	**onion,** *quartered*	
1	**carrot,** *sliced*	
1	**bay leaf**	
1	**small, dried hot pepper**	
2 sprigs	**coriander**	
6	**peppercorns**	
½ cup	**Coriander-Lime Vinaigrette** *(recipe on p. 95)*	125 ml
	watercress *or* **other crisp greens**	
1	**ripe avocado**	
2	**green onions,** *finely chopped*	
12	**cherry tomatoes**	
¼ cup	**fresh coriander,** *chopped*	60 ml

Serve this south-of-the-border-inspired salad with warm crisp tortilla wedges and icy bottles of Mexican beer.

1. Bring several inches of water to a boil in a large, shallow pan with the onion, carrot, bay leaf, hot pepper, coriander sprigs, and peppercorns. Simmer for about 15 minutes.

2. Slip in the chicken breasts, cover the pan, and simmer 5–10 minutes, until meat is tender and juices run clear. Keep the chicken in the pan and set aside to cool in the liquid.

3. Remove skin and bones from chicken, and cut or shred the meat into bite-sized pieces. Toss with ¼ cup (60 ml) of Coriander-Lime Vinaigrette and refrigerate until ready to serve.

4. At serving time, line a platter with watercress or greens and arrange avocado slices on top. Drizzle with another few tablespoons of the Coriander-Lime Vinaigrette. Pile chicken in the centre and circle with halved cherry tomatoes. Scatter chopped green onions and chopped coriander on top.

Serves 4.

TIPS:

• Poaching the chicken keeps it moist; the basic method described here can be varied to suit the flavouring ingredients you have on hand.

• Steps 1–3 can be done early in the day of serving; you can even poach the chicken the day before and combine it with the vinaigrette the next morning.

White Bean & Sausage Salad

1 clove	**garlic,** *minced*	
1/3 cup	**olive oil**	**75 ml**
2 tbsp	**red wine vinegar**	**30 ml**
	salt and freshly ground pepper	
2 tbsp	**fresh mint,** *chopped*	**30 ml**
1 can	**white beans** *(19 oz/540 ml)* **or**	
2 cups	**cooked white beans** *(directions on p.110)*	**500 ml**
1/2	**small red onion,** *slivered*	
1 lb	**hot** *or* **sweet Italian sausage** *or* **chorizo**	**500 g**
4	**firm, ripe tomatoes**	

TIP:

• This salad is also delicious with tuna instead of sausage: Reserve some of the dressing before tossing it with the beans and add a squeeze of lemon juice. Toss chunks of barbecued fresh tuna or canned tuna with this dressing. Omit the sausage, and add the tuna to the beans at serving time with a handful of ripe Italian olives.

Traditionally, mint is used to flavour this salad from southern Italy, but if you don't have a supply of fresh mint, use basil or thyme instead. Simply omit the sausage for a lighter, vegetarian salad.

1. Make dressing: Combine garlic with salt, pepper, vinegar, 1/4 cup (60 ml) of the oil, and half the mint.

2. Combine beans and onion, and toss gently with the dressing.

3. Simmer the sausage in 1/2" (2 cm) of water in a covered skillet for 10 minutes. Drain and continue cooking in the skillet, or grill on the barbecue, until nicely browned. Cool, cut into thin slices, and add to the beans. Refrigerate until serving time.

4. Just before serving, peel, seed, and cut the tomatoes in chunks, then toss with the rest of the oil and the mint, and season to taste.

5. Mound the bean mixture on a platter and circle with tomatoes. Serve at room temperature with hot crusty bread to mop up the good juices.

Serves 4.

Basic Vinaigrette

1 clove	garlic, *crushed*	
1 tsp	Dijon mustard, *smooth or grainy*	5 ml
2 tbsp	red wine vinegar	30 ml
	salt and freshly ground pepper	
6 tbsp	olive oil	90 ml

Roasted Tomato Vinaigrette

1	plum tomato	
½ tsp	ground cumin	2 ml
pinch	cayenne	
	salt and freshly ground pepper	
½ cup	extra-virgin olive oil	125 ml
¼ cup	balsamic vinegar, *or* half lemon juice, half vinegar	60 ml

A Quartet of Vinaigrettes

Basic Vinaigrette

Make double the recipe of this vinaigrette for the Salade Niçoise (p. 102).

1. In a small bowl, combine garlic, a dash of salt, mustard, and vinegar. Whisk in oil, then add pepper. Or combine ingredients in a small jar, cover, and shake until smooth.

2. Taste and adjust seasoning, adding a dash more vinegar or oil to suit your taste.

Makes about ½ cup (125 ml).

Roasted Tomato Vinaigrette

Use this vinaigrette with Roasted Vegetable Couscous (p. 112).

1. Cut the tomato in half and rub with olive oil, salt, and pepper. Set on the grill over low heat for about 10–12 minutes, turning once.

2. Peel blackened skin off tomato and squeeze out seeds. You should have about 1 tbsp (15 ml) of pulp.

3. Add cumin, cayenne, and salt and pepper to the pulp and pound to a paste. Whisk in vinegar and olive oil.

Makes about ¾ cup (175 ml).

Lemon-Cumin Vinaigrette

1/4 tsp	salt	1 ml
1 clove	garlic, *crushed*	
1/2 tsp	cumin	2 ml
1/2 tsp	dried oregano	2 ml
pinch	cayenne	
2 tbsp	fresh lemon juice	30 ml
6 tbsp	olive oil	90 ml

Basil Vinaigrette

1 cup	fresh basil leaves (packed) or	250 ml
2 tbsp	Basil Purée (see Tip, p. 103)	30 ml
2–3 tbsp	balsamic *or* sherry vinegar	30–45 ml
6 tbsp	olive oil	90 ml
	salt and freshly ground pepper	

Lemon-Cumin Vinaigrette

Use this dressing on Moroccan Lentil Salad (p. 104) and Lemon-Cumin Couscous Salad (p. 113).

1. Combine the salt, garlic, cumin, oregano, cayenne, and lemon juice. Whisk in oil.

Makes about 1/2 cup (125 ml).

Basil Vinaigrette

Basil and tomatoes are meant for each other – try this dressing on a sliced tomato salad and the Tri-Colour Pasta Salad (p. 103).

1. Purée the basil in a food processor with the vinegar, then blend in oil and seasonings. (Or chop the basil leaves finely by hand and pound to a paste with a little salt before mixing with the rest of the ingredients.) Alternatively, combine Basil Purée with other ingredients in a small jar and shake well.

Makes about 2/3 cup (150 ml).

TIPS:

• A vinaigrette is a combination of an oil, an acid, and flavouring ingredients. The basic balance – although it's certainly a matter of personal taste – is 3 or 4 parts oil to 1 part acid. Salads with legumes and grains can take more acid.

• Have an assortment of oils and vinegars on hand so you can try different combinations: For greens, choose a light olive, safflower, or corn oil, and a lighter wine vinegar such as champagne or sweetly pungent balsamic vinegar. Olive oil and red wine vinegar work well with robust vegetable, pasta, and grain salads.

• If you're using the vinaigrette on a basic green salad, add 1 shallot or 2 green onions, finely chopped, and 1–2 tbsp (15–30 ml) chopped fresh parsley and chives to the dressing just before tossing the salad.

• 1/2 cup (125 ml) vinaigrette makes enough to dress salad for 6–8.

• If the flavour of the vinegar is too raw and assertive, simply add a pinch of sugar.

Salade Niçoise

1 lb	**potatoes,** *cooked, cooled, and cut in chunks*	500 g
1 lb	**green beans,** *blanched and cooled*	500 g
4	**firm, ripe tomatoes,** *quartered*	
1 can	**chunk tuna,** *drained (6.5 oz/184 g)*	
3	**hard-boiled eggs,** *quartered*	
1 can	**anchovy fillets** *(2 oz/50 g)*	
½ cup	**black olives**	125 ml
	fresh herbs, *chopped (a combination such as parsley, chives, and thyme*	
3	**green onions,** *diced*	
1 cup	**Basic Vinaigrette** *(recipe on p. 100)*	250 ml
1 head	**lettuce**	

TIPS:

•Substitute lightly steamed asparagus spears for the green beans.

• Use spinach or arugula leaves instead of lettuce.

A popular lunch-time salad, open to variation according to the supply of ingredients and the numbers to be fed. Serve with warm, crusty French bread.

1. Toss potatoes with about ¹/₂ cup (125 ml) of Basic Vinaigrette; set aside.

2. Just before serving, line a platter with lettuce. Season beans and tomatoes with a little more Basic Vinaigrette. Arrange potatoes in the centre of the platter. Surround with beans and tomatoes and decorate with tuna, eggs, anchovy fillets, and olives. Sprinkle with onions, herbs, and a little more vinaigrette.

Serves 4 for lunch.

TIPS:

•Salad greens with soft-textured leaves, such as Bibb lettuce and Boston lettuce, spoil very quickly. Romaine, iceberg, and leaf and red-leaf lettuce travel better and hold up longer.

• Greens with sharper flavour such as watercress, radicchio, endive, escarole, and spinach also keep well.

Tri-Colour Pasta Salad

½ lb	fusilli or rotini	250 g
⅔ cup	**Basil Vinaigrette** (*recipe on p. 101*)	150 ml
½	**medium red onion,** *quartered and thinly sliced*	
1 each	**red and yellow pepper,** *roasted and sliced (see p. 91)*	
½ lb	**green beans**	250 g
8–10	**cherry tomatoes,** *halved*	
	salt and freshly ground pepper	
handful	**black olives** (*optional*)	
	fresh flat-leaf parsley *or* **basil,** *chopped (if available)*	

Every mouthful tastes of summer. The salad can be varied to take advantage of the vegetables you have on hand.

1. Cook pasta in a large pot of boiling, salted water until just tender – test after 8 minutes. Drain, refresh under cold water, and drain thoroughly again. Turn into a large bowl.

2. While pasta is still warm, toss with ⅓ cup (75 ml) of Basil Vinaigrette. Add sliced red onion and peppers.

3. Snip stem ends from beans, drop into a large pot of boiling, salted water, and cook for 5 minutes. Drain and drop into ice water to stop cooking. Drain again, cover, and refrigerate until needed.

4. When ready to serve the salad, cut beans in half and toss beans and halved tomatoes with another ⅓ cup (75 ml) of Basil Vinaigrette. Finally, add beans and tomatoes to the pasta and toss everything together. Season to taste and garnish with olives and parsley or basil.

Serves 6.

TIPS:

• Steps 1–3 can be done ahead. Store, covered, in the refrigerator. Since green beans lose their crispness and fresh colour when left too long in vinegar dressing, and tomatoes become soft and watery, toss them in dressing and add to the pasta just before serving.

• Add chunks of tuna to make a main-dish salad.

• This salad is also delicious with other grilled summer vegetables such as zucchini and eggplant. (See pp. 90–91.)

TIP:

• Since fresh basil doesn't keep very long, this purée is very handy: Rinse and dry several bunches of basil, then strip the leaves from the stalks. Put them in the bowl of a blender or food processor with a spoon or two of olive oil. Use on/off pulses until the basil is uniformly chopped. Spoon purée into small containers and add a thin film of olive oil to cover the surface. Will keep fresh for a week in the refrigerator or several months in the freezer.

Moroccan Lentil Salad

1½ cups	small brown or green lentils	375 ml
1	medium carrot, *diced*	
1	bay leaf	
	leaves from 1 stalk celery	
½	medium red onion, *finely chopped*	
1	red pepper, *roasted, seeded, and diced (for roasting directions, see p. 91)*	
¼ cup	flat-leaf parsley, *chopped*	60 ml
1–2 tbsp	fresh coriander, *chopped (if available)*	15–30 ml
½ cup	Lemon-Cumin Vinaigrette *(recipe on p. 101)*	125 ml

This salad is excellent to take on a picnic. It travels well, and the flavour gets better the longer it sits.

1. Pick over lentils to remove stones and debris, and rinse. Toss into a large quantity of salted water with carrot, bay leaf, and celery leaves. Bring to a boil and cook over moderate heat until just tender. Cooking time varies; start testing the lentils after 20 minutes so you don't overcook. Drain and rinse under cold water.

2. While lentils are still warm, combine with remaining ingredients and ½ cup (125 ml) Lemon-Cumin Vinaigrette. Cover and refrigerate for a while to allow flavours to blend. Serve at room temperature.

Serves 6.

TIP:
• This salad will keep 2–3 days in the fridge.

Summer Squash Salad

2 lbs	**small summer squash** (*zucchini, yellow, and/or pattypan*)	1 kg
	Basic Vinaigrette (*recipe on p. 100*)	
1	**shallot** or	
2	**green onions,** *finely chopped*	
1 tbsp	**fresh dill,** *chopped*	15 ml

TIP:

•To prevent summer squash from becoming waterlogged when blanched or cooked, drop them into a large pot of boiling, salted water without trimming the stem or blossom ends. Simply wipe them with a damp cloth first.

This quickly prepared side dish is light and refreshing and has a pleasing crunch.

1. Make Basic Vinaigrette using olive oil and equal parts fresh lemon juice and balsamic vinegar.

2. Cook whole squash, untrimmed, for 4–5 minutes, then drop briefly into ice water to stop further cooking. Drain and pat dry.

3. Trim off stem and blossom ends, cut each squash in half lengthwise, and then cut each half crosswise into 1" (2.5-cm) chunks.

4. Toss with vinaigrette and remaining ingredients while still warm. Cover and refrigerate. Serve at room temperature.

Serves 6–8.

Mediterranean Potato Salad

2 lbs	potatoes	1 kg
½ cup	dry white wine	125 ml
	salt and freshly ground pepper	
½	medium red onion, *finely sliced*	
½ cup	ripe black olives, *pitted and chopped*	125 ml
4	green onions, *finely chopped*	
¼ cup	softened sun-dried tomatoes, *chopped*	60 ml
½ cup	Basic Vinaigrette *(recipe on p. 100)*	125 ml
½ cup	fresh parsley, *chopped*	125 ml

TIP:

• Remember this rough guideline: Buy round potatoes for boiling and long oval ones for baking and frying. Round ones have a higher moisture content and hold their shape when boiled. Long, oval potatoes will disintegrate.

This variation of the classic summer salad is great for picnics because it's made without mayonnaise and consequently travels well. Use firm-textured potatoes – one of the red-skinned varieties, for instance, or small new potatoes. Whether you leave the skins on or take them off depends on your preference and on the newness of the potatoes.

1. Cover potatoes in salted water and boil until just tender. (Test them after 15 minutes.) Drain, remove skins if desired, and chop into smallish chunks. Sprinkle with wine and seasonings.

2. Add red onion, olives, sun-dried tomatoes, and green onions, and toss with vinaigrette.

3. Set aside at room temperature for about an hour for flavours to blend. Toss again with chopped fresh parsley before serving.

Serves 6.

TIPS:

• Try adding slivers of roasted red, green, or yellow peppers; quartered, marinated artichoke hearts; thinly sliced radishes; or a handful of chopped sharp fresh greens such as arugula, endive, or sorrel.

• To make a main-dish salad, add tuna, whole cooked shrimp, or slices of grilled Italian sausage.

• Hot potatoes absorb flavours well; cold ones don't. Therefore, when making a potato salad with a vinaigrette, toss potatoes in the dressing while they are still hot.

Green & Yellow Beans
with Honey-Mustard Dressing

½ lb	each green and	250 g
	yellow wax beans	
	Honey-Mustard Dressing	

Honey-Mustard Dressing

3 tbsp	Dijon mustard	45 ml
3 tbsp	honey	45 ml
	juice of 1 lemon	
3 tbsp	white wine vinegar	45 ml
½ cup	light olive oil *or* vegetable oil	125 ml
½ cup	fresh dill, *chopped*	125 ml
	salt and freshly ground pepper	

TIPS:

• Steps 1 and 2 may be done the day before. Store, covered, in the fridge.

• Beans lose their fresh colour when left too long in a vinaigrette, so combine them with the dressing just prior to serving.

• The Honey-Mustard Dressing will keep 2–3 days in a covered jar in the refrigerator. It will keep for several weeks if you omit the fresh dill and mix it in just before serving.

Beans never taste any better than during the summer months, when they are freshly picked. The Honey-Mustard Dressing is guaranteed to become a favourite; try it as a dip with asparagus or other fresh vegetables, or serve alongside cold salmon.

1. Snip the stem ends off the beans and toss in a large pot of lightly salted, boiling water. Cook until just tender, tasting after 5 minutes. (Cooking time will vary depending on the size and freshness of the beans.)

2. Dump beans into ice water to stop the cooking, and drain well.

3. Just before serving, toss beans with enough Honey-Mustard Dressing to coat them lightly. (You won't need all the dressing.)

Serves 4.

Honey-Mustard Dressing
1. Combine ingredients well.

Makes about 1 cup (250 ml).

Tabbouleh with a Twist

1 cup	**fine bulgur**	250 ml
4	**green onions,** *chopped*	
4	**tomatoes,** *seeded and finely chopped*	
1 bunch	**fresh parsley,** *finely chopped*	
1 bunch	**fresh mint,** *finely chopped*	
½	**green pepper,** *chopped*	
½	**English cucumber,** *finely chopped*	
2 cups	**feta cheese,** *cubed*	500 ml
1 can	**chick peas,** *rinsed and drained (19 oz/540 ml)*	
2	**carrots,** *grated*	
⅔ cup	**olive oil**	150 ml
½ cup	**fresh lemon juice**	125 ml
2 tsp	**minced garlic**	10 ml
	salt and freshly ground pepper	

This version of the traditional Middle Eastern salad contains feta cheese, which gives it a delicious tangy taste. It's a great summer salad because it can be made ahead, is easily transported, and is even better the second day – if there's any left.

1. Soak bulgur in hot water to cover for 20 minutes. Drain well, pressing out excess water.

2. Add remaining salad ingredients to bulgur in a large bowl.

3. Combine olive oil, lemon juice, garlic, and salt and pepper in a jar with a tight-fitting lid, and shake to blend. Pour over salad and toss until well mixed.

Serves 6–8.

TIPS:

• Bulgur (a nutty-tasting cracked wheat) is available at bulk-food stores and many supermarkets.

• For traditional tabbouleh, omit the feta, chick peas, and carrots.

• The flavour improves with standing time, so prepare ahead if possible.

• Prepare the salad substituting 1½ cups (375 ml) couscous for the bulgur. Couscous has a different flavour and texture, and makes for a lighter salad. (See p. 113 for directions on preparing couscous.)

Tabbouleh is great for a picnic or potluck since it travels well. You can leave out the feta cheese and chick peas if you don't have them on hand.

Corn & Black Bean Salsa

1 can	**black beans, rinsed and drained,** (19 oz/540 ml) **or**	
2 cups	**cooked black beans** (see below)	500 ml
2 ears	**corn**	
1	**large, ripe tomato,** seeded and chopped	
1	**red pepper,** roasted, peeled, seeded, and chopped	
1 tbsp	**jalapeño pepper,** chopped (fresh or canned)	15 ml
1–2 cloves	**garlic,** finely chopped	
2	**green onions,** finely chopped	
	juice of 1 lime	
1 tbsp	**olive oil**	15 ml
dash	**hot sauce**	
	salt and freshly ground pepper	
¼ cup	**fresh coriander** or **Italian parsley,** chopped	60 ml

Cooking the corn on the grill adds a light smoky taste to this colourful vegetable mixture. Serve it as a before-dinner snack with crisp corn chips, or as a side dish with grilled chicken, pork, or fish.

1. Cook corn on grill. (See p. 90 for method.)

2. Remove kernels from the cobs and combine with remaining ingredients. Let mixture stand an hour or so in the refrigerator for flavours to blend. Taste and adjust seasoning.

Makes 3 cups (750 ml).

TIPS:

• The salsa will keep 2–3 days in the refrigerator. If you plan to make it ahead, add the green onion and fresh herbs on the day of serving.

• There is a wicked-looking tool with a curved blade for speedily removing corn kernels from the cobs, but a good, sharp knife works just as well. Hold the blade at a slight angle and draw it firmly down against the cob.

HOW TO COOK BEANS:

• To cook dried beans using the quick-soak method, rinse and pick through the beans to remove any debris. Place beans in a large saucepan and cover with cold water. Cover pan and bring to a boil. Remove from heat and set aside for an hour. (Alternatively, instead of boiling, leave beans in cold water to soak overnight.) Drain, rinse beans, and cover with fresh, cold water. Add some flavourings if you like (an onion studded with 2 cloves and a bay leaf, for example). Gently bring to a boil, lower heat, and cook, covered, until tender – about 1½ hours.

• 1 cup (250 ml) dried beans equals 2–2½ cups (500–625 ml) cooked beans.

Pico de Gallo

4	**large, ripe tomatoes,** *diced*	
1	**small onion,** *diced*	
2	**cloves garlic,** *minced*	
2–3	**fresh jalapeño peppers,** *finely chopped, veins and seeds removed*	
3 tbsp	**fresh coriander** *or* **flat-leaf parsley,** *finely chopped*	45 ml
1 tbsp	**fresh basil,** *chopped* **or**	15 ml
½ tsp	**dried basil**	2 ml
2 tbsp	**fresh lime juice**	30 ml
2 tbsp	**safflower** *or* **olive oil**	30 ml
	salt	

TIP:

• If the flavour of fresh coriander is not to your taste (or if none is available), use Italian flat-leaf parsley.

Pico de Gallo is a refreshing relish that tastes best when freshly made. (Luckily, it takes only minutes to prepare.) It's an essential topping for fajitas (see p. 48) and a good accompaniment to grilled fish, but it's also great just served as a snack with corn chips.

1. Combine all ingredients. Toss lightly.

Makes 2 cups (500 ml).

TIPS:

• Some field tomatoes have thin skins, and peeling them is a matter of choice. Others, like the plum varieties, have tough skins that require peeling. A proven technique is to have a pot of water boiling on the stove. Drop in a tomato and count to 10. Lift the tomato out, and drop into cold water or hold under the tap. Cut a cross on the smooth end and the skin will slip off in large sections. Cut out the core at the stem end. The process takes about 10 seconds, so slip another tomato into the pot as you take one out.

Roasted Vegetable Couscous

1	**medium eggplant,** *sliced*	
2	**zucchini,** *sliced*	
1	**large onion,** *sliced or cut in eighths*	
2	**sweet peppers,** *seeded and cut in quarters*	
2 cloves	**garlic,** *finely chopped*	
4 tbsp	**olive oil**	60 ml
¾ cup	**Roasted Tomato Vinaigrette** *(recipe on p. 100)*	175 ml
1 cup	**couscous**	250 ml
1 cup	**hot vegetable** *or* **chicken stock**	250 ml
1 tbsp	**lemon juice**	15 ml
4 oz	**feta** *or* **goat cheese,** *crumbled*	125 g
	salt and freshly ground pepper	
	parsley, *finely chopped*	

This salad has everything going for it. It travels well, is infinitely variable using the summer vegetables you have on hand, and is easily made ahead. It's an excellent side dish with any grilled food, and a great main dish for a picnic when piled into pita-bread pockets. Just pack it in a plastic container for travelling, then spoon it into the pita breads when it's time to eat.

1. Toss vegetables with garlic and 3 tbsp (45 ml) of the oil, and a little salt and pepper.

2. Arrange vegetables on a preheated barbecue and grill for about 5–10 minutes per side until tender and lightly browned. *Note: A roasted plum tomato is required for the vinaigrette (see p. 100), so grill it at the same time as the other vegetables.*

3. Meanwhile, place couscous in a large bowl, cover with hot stock, and leave for 5 minutes. When all the liquid is absorbed, fluff grains with a fork. Liven flavour with the lemon juice and remaining olive oil.

4. Cut the vegetables into small pieces and toss with couscous and Roasted Tomato Vinaigrette. Season to taste and scatter cheese and parsley on top.

Serves 4–6.

TIPS:

• For a great pasta salad, substitute 2 cups (500 ml) cooked penne for the couscous.

• The vegetables can also be roasted in the oven: Spread in a single layer in a large roasting pan and roast on the top rack of the oven at 475°F (240°C) for 30–40 minutes, turning a few times, until lightly browned and just tender.

Lemon-Cumin Couscous Salad

1½ cups	hot water *or* light stock	375 ml
1½ cups	couscous	375 ml
¼ cup	lemon juice	60 ml
2 tbsp	olive oil	30 ml
4	green onions, *finely chopped*	
½ cup	raisins	125 ml
½ cup	dried apricots, *chopped*	125 ml
½ cup	parsley, *finely chopped*	125 ml
½ cup	slivered almonds, *toasted*	125 ml
½ cup	Lemon-Cumin Vinaigrette *(recipe on p. 101)*	125 ml
	salt and freshly ground pepper	

Couscous (flour-coated semolina) can be combined with various flavourings to make great-tasting side-dish salads that keep well. This light, fruity version goes well with Honey-Lime Pork Loin (p. 86) or Chicken Satay (p. 58).

1. Place couscous in a large bowl and cover with the hot water or stock. When all the liquid is absorbed (about 5 minutes), fluff grains with a fork and liven the flavour with lemon juice and olive oil.

2. Toss with remaining ingredients and the Lemon-Cumin Vinaigrette. Cover and refrigerate to allow flavours to blend.

3. Taste and adjust seasoning, adding additional lemon juice or a splash of oil as necessary before serving.

Serves 6–8.

TIPS:

• Couscous is available at bulk-food stores. Precooked couscous can now be found in many supermarkets; read the preparation instructions on the package.

• Grain salads absorb liquid and flavour as they stand. Prepare ahead for the best flavour and have a little extra dressing, lemon juice, or balsamic vinegar on hand for last-minute seasoning.

• This salad travels well, and keeps for 2–3 days in the refrigerator. If making a day or more ahead, add parsley and nuts at serving time to preserve fresh taste and crunch.

Raspberry-Spinach Salad

Almond Topping

1/2 cup	slivered almonds	125 ml
1/4 cup	granulated sugar	60 ml
2 tsp	water	10 ml

Dressing

1/4 cup	granulated sugar	60 ml
1 1/2 tbsp	poppy seeds	25 ml
1/4 tsp	paprika	1 ml
1/2 cup	vegetable oil	125 ml
1/4 cup	raspberry vinegar	60 ml
2 tsp	onion, *finely chopped*	10 ml
1/4 tsp	Worcestershire sauce	1 ml

Salad

1 lb	fresh spinach	500 g
2 cups	fresh raspberries	500 ml

Crunchy caramelized almonds add the crowning touch to this simple, beautiful-looking, and delicious summer salad.

1. Combine topping ingredients in a large frying pan. Cook over medium heat, stirring constantly, until sugar melts to a golden brown and coats almonds, about 5 minutes. Turn out onto a square of greased foil. Cool, then break up into small pieces.

2. Combine all dressing ingredients in a container with a tight-fitting lid. Shake well to blend, then shake again before using.

3. Wash and dry spinach, and place in a large bowl with raspberries. Add dressing and toss. Add almonds; toss lightly and serve immediately.

Serves 4.

TIP:

• **Prepare a few batches of almonds and dressing ahead of time and keep on hand. Hide the topping in a safe place, though, or it may disappear.**

Raspberry-Spinach Salad: It looks impressive, but is easy to prepare. Make the caramelized almonds ahead of time.

Tomato & Feta Salad

3	large, firm, ripe tomatoes	
½	small cucumber	
3 tbsp	balsamic vinegar or	45 ml
2 tbsp	red wine vinegar	30 ml
¼ cup	olive oil	60 ml
	salt and freshly ground pepper	
1 tbsp	fresh oregano, *chopped* or	15 ml
1 tsp	dried oregano	5 ml
1 tbsp	fresh parsley, *chopped*	15 ml
¼ cup	green onion, *chopped*	60 ml
1 clove	garlic, *finely chopped*	
½ cup	feta cheese, *crumbled*	125 ml
	black olives *(optional)*	

When local tomatoes are at their best, it's hard to beat this simple salad.

1. Slice the tomatoes and arrange in a slightly overlapping single layer in a shallow serving dish. Season lightly.

2. Peel the cucumber, slice lengthwise, scoop out seeds, and chop.

3. Combine vinegar, oil, salt, and pepper. Toss half the dressing with the cucumber pieces, herbs, garlic, and green onion, and spread over tomatoes.

4. Top with crumbled feta cheese and a few black olives, if you like. Pour remaining dressing over the top.

Serves 6.

TIPS:

• Substitute slices of fresh mozzarella for the feta and intersperse with the tomato slices. Replace oregano with fresh basil.

• Store tomatoes in a cool, airy spot. Refrigerators are too cold and cause tomatoes to become "grainy" and lose their flavour.

Greek Salad

½ head	**romaine lettuce**	
2	**large tomatoes,** *sliced* **or**	
1 pint	**cherry tomatoes,** *halved*	
1	**green pepper,** *sliced in thin rings*	
½	**red onion,** *sliced in thin rings*	
½ cup	**feta cheese,** *crumbled*	125 ml
1 tbsp	**red wine vinegar** *or* **lemon juice**	15 ml
3 tbsp	**olive oil**	45 ml
1 tsp	**dried oregano**	5 ml
2 tbsp	**flat-leaf parsley,** *chopped*	30 ml
½ cup	**black olives,** *pitted and sliced*	125 ml
	salt and freshly ground pepper	

This salad goes well with any Mediterranean-flavoured grilled fish or meat, and it's the perfect topping for a Greek Burger (p. 76). Just pile whatever parts of the salad take your fancy into a pita bread on top of the burger.

1. Tear up lettuce leaves and line a large platter with them.

2. Arrange layers of tomato slices and green pepper and onion rings on the lettuce. Top with crumbled feta cheese.

3. Whisk together olive oil, lemon juice or vinegar, and salt and pepper, and drizzle over salad.

4. Sprinkle oregano, parsley, and olives on top and add a dash more pepper.

Serves 6.

Napa Cabbage Salad

Napa cabbage, also called Chinese cabbage, looks like a long, celery-shaped head of cabbage, and goes well with the Oriental flavours in this wonderful salad. The recipe is great for a crowd but can easily be halved.

1. Several hours before using, mix together the soup flavour packets from the noodles, oil, vinegar, sugar, and salt. Stir occasionally.

2. Chop the cabbage. (You should have about 16 cups/4 L.) Add the onions and parsley.

3. Mix dressing thoroughly with salad greens. Just before serving, add sesame seeds, almonds, and dry soup noodles, slightly crushed. Toss to mix.

Serves 15.

2 pkgs	**Oriental instant noodles with chicken** *or* **beef-flavoured soup base** *(85–100 g each)*	
1 cup	**vegetable oil**	**250 ml**
6 tbsp	**rice vinegar** *or* **balsamic** *or* **white wine vinegar**	**90 ml**
4 tsp	**granulated sugar**	**20 ml**
2 tsp	**salt**	**10 ml**
1	**large Napa cabbage** *(10"/25 cm long)*	
8	**green onions**, *chopped*	
½ cup	**fresh parsley**, *chopped*	**125 ml**
1 cup	**sliced almonds**, *toasted*	**250 ml**
½ cup	**sesame seeds**, *toasted*	**125 ml**

TIPS:

• A small, diced red pepper adds a nice touch of colour.

• If Napa cabbage is unavailable, you can substitute finely shredded regular green cabbage.

TIPS:

• Toast almonds and sesame seeds on shallow baking pan at 375°F (190°C) for 3–6 minutes, stirring often until golden brown.

• Salad can be prepared the day before. Add sesame seeds, almonds, and noodles just before serving.

Gazpacho Salad

2	**large tomatoes,** *seeded and diced*	
½	**cucumber,** *diced (about 4"/10 cm)*	
½ each	**red and green pepper,** *diced*	
1	**small red onion,** *finely chopped*	
1 clove	**garlic,** *minced*	
½ cup	**fresh parsley,** *or* **part parsley, part coriander,** *chopped*	**125 ml**
2 tbsp	**balsamic vinegar,** *or* **half vinegar, half lemon juice**	**30 ml**
2 tbsp	**olive oil**	**30 ml**
	salt and freshly ground pepper	

Serve this crunchy salad all by itself or as a topping for burgers or Brazilian Mini-Meatball-Stuffed Pitas (p. 154). Add cubed feta cheese and a handful of black olives and it becomes a complete dish that can be tucked into pita breads.

1. In a large bowl, combine all ingredients and toss well. Keep cool until serving.

Serves 4–6.

TIP:

• To remove seeds from a tomato, cut in half horizontally, loosen seeds with your fingers, and squeeze gently. Or slice into 8 segments and release the seeds from each section.

• Remove the stem end from large tomatoes; they are often tough and woody, and can spoil a salad or sauce.

Brown Rice Salad

1½ cups	brown rice, *rinsed*	375 ml
½ lb	green beans *or* snow *or* sugar snap peas *or* asparagus	250 g
½	each red and green peppers, *diced*	
1 can	water chestnuts, *rinsed and sliced* (8 oz/227 ml)	
2	green onions, *finely chopped*	
1	orange (*optional*)	
1 cup	roasted peanuts, *chopped*	250 ml
2 tbsp	fresh coriander *or* **parsley**, *chopped*	30 ml
	Orange–Soy Dressing	

Orange–Soy Dressing

¼ cup	orange juice	60 ml
¼ cup	lemon juice	60 ml
3 tbsp	soy sauce	45 ml
3 tbsp	brown sugar	45 ml
½ cup	vegetable oil	125 ml
½ tsp	chile flakes	2 ml
	salt and freshly ground pepper	

This salad travels well on summer outings. Enjoy it beside chicken or pork satays (p. 58), Ginger-Mango Shrimp Kebabs (p. 85), or Honey-Lime Pork Loin Roast (p. 86).

1. Cook rice in a large pot of lightly salted boiling water until tender, about 20–25 minutes. Drain well.

2. Blanch the green beans, snow or snap peas, or asparagus, and cut on the diagonal into ½" (1-cm) pieces. Grate the orange zest and divide the orange into segments.

3. While the rice is still warm, toss with a spoonful or two of dressing. Cool, then mix in all the remaining ingredients. Add more dressing as required and season to taste. Garnish with some extra chopped peanuts and chopped coriander or parsley sprinkled on top.

Serves 4–6.

Orange–Soy Dressing

1. Mix ingredients together well. Taste and adjust seasoning.

Makes about 1¼ cups (300 ml).

TIPS:

• Salad will keep in a tightly covered container in the refrigerator for about 2 days.

• Rice salad absorbs dressing as it sits in the refrigerator. Sprinkle with extra dressing if needed.

Couscous-Stuffed Tomatoes

6	firm, ripe tomatoes	
½ cup	couscous	125 ml
1 tbsp	lemon juice	15 ml
2 tbsp	olive oil	30 ml
1	small onion, *finely chopped*	
1 clove	garlic, *minced*	
1 tsp	cumin	5 ml
½ tsp	oregano	2 ml
pinch	cayenne	
2 tbsp	currants	30 ml
¼ cup	parsley, *chopped*	60 ml
¼ cup	pine nuts, *toasted*	60 ml
	salt and freshly ground pepper	

TIP:

•The tomatoes can also be baked on the grill: Set them in a foil dish, cover with foil, and cook over medium heat with the lid closed following Step 6.

A tasty side dish with food from the grill, or a good main dish for a light vegetarian lunch or dinner.

1. Cut the tops off the tomatoes about ¹/₂" (1 cm) down. Scoop out the insides with a small spoon. Discard seeds, but save and chop the pulp.

2. Lightly salt the inside of each tomato and set upside down on paper towels to drain.

3. Meanwhile, prepare stuffing: Heat lemon juice with a scant cup (235 ml) water until boiling, and pour over couscous. Leave until liquid is absorbed (about 5 minutes), then fluff with a fork.

4. In a small frying pan, cook the onion in oil until soft; add garlic, reserved tomato pulp, and seasonings. Cook gently for about 10 minutes.

5. Remove from heat, stir in currants, parsley, and pine nuts, and season to taste. Lightly toss mixture into couscous.

6. When ready to bake, season insides of tomatoes, spoon in stuffing, and drizzle a little extra olive oil on top. Set in a baking dish, cover with foil, and bake at 350°F (180°C) for 15 minutes. Remove foil and continue baking until the tomatoes are tender and the stuffing is nicely brown – about 10 minutes more. (Don't overcook.) Serve hot or at room temperature.

Serves 6.

Garlic Roast Potatoes

2 –2½ lbs	**potatoes**	**1–1.25 kg**
3 tbsp	**olive oil** *or* **half butter, half oil**	**45 ml**
3 cloves	**garlic,** *finely chopped*	
	salt and freshly ground pepper	

This simple dish can be varied by adding a sprinkling of your favourite fresh or dried herbs to the roasting potatoes. Fresh rosemary and oregano are good choices when the potatoes are being served with lamb; thyme works well with pork or beef. Or try a spice such as cumin or garam masala.

1. Scrub potatoes (leave skins on) and cut into 1½" (4-cm) chunks. Heat oil (or oil and butter) with the garlic in a shallow roasting pan in a 450°F (230°C) oven.

2. Toss the potato chunks into the hot oil. Roast for about 30 minutes, turning the potatoes now and again so they become brown and crispy on all sides.

3. Sprinkle with salt and pepper and serve at once.

Serves 6.

TIP:
• Sprinkle the potato chunks with 2 tbsp (30 ml) of fresh chopped herbs or 2 tsp (10 ml) dried herbs when adding them to the hot oil.

Potatoes Savoyard

2 lbs	**potatoes,** *peeled and* thinly sliced ⅛" (3 mm) thick	**1 kg**
	salt and freshly ground pepper	
3 tbsp	**butter**	**45 ml**
1 clove	**garlic,** *minced*	
2 cups	**Gruyère cheese,** *grated*	**500 ml**
1 cup	**beef** *or* **chicken stock**	**250 ml**

This classic recipe comes from the Savoie region of France, where potatoes are baked with stock in place of milk or cream, as in the familiar scalloped-potato dish. It goes well with most main courses, but is especially good with grilled or roasted meats.

1. Lightly butter a shallow 9" x 13" (23-cm x 33-cm) baking dish. Cover the bottom of the dish with a slightly overlapping layer of thin potato slices. Season with salt and pepper, dot with a third of the butter, add a little garlic, and sprinkle with a third of the cheese.

2. Repeat the layers, finishing with butter and cheese.

3. Pour the stock over top. Bake in a 425°F (220°C) oven for 30 minutes. Tilt the dish and spoon the cooking juices over the potatoes.

4. Lower the heat to 350°F (180°C) and continue cooking until potatoes are tender and the top is nicely browned, about 20–30 minutes more.

Serves 6.

TIP:

• Use a mature all-purpose variety of potato such as Yukon Gold; moist, waxy varieties do not absorb the cooking liquid as well and tend to stay too firm.

Layered Cheesy Potatoes

2 lbs	**potatoes,** *peeled and thinly sliced*	1 kg
¼ cup	**olive oil**	60 ml
½ tsp	**dried thyme**	2 ml
½ tsp	**dried oregano**	2 ml
1	**medium red onion,** *sliced*	
1–2 cloves	**garlic,** *finely chopped*	
	salt and freshly ground pepper	
1	**large, ripe tomato,** *thinly sliced*	
1 cup	**mozzarella,** *grated*	250 ml

Served hot or at room temperature, this is a good accompaniment to grilled or roasted meats. It can also be served hot as a vegetarian main dish with a salad.

1. Dry potato slices with paper towels or a cloth.

2. Heat 2 tbsp (30 ml) of the oil in a frying pan. Add onion and a pinch or two of the herbs. Cook for a few minutes over medium/high heat until slightly softened and beginning to brown. Add garlic, salt, and pepper.

3. Lightly oil a shallow 9" x 13" (23-cm x 33-cm) baking dish and spoon in half the onion and garlic mixture.

4. Add a layer of half the potato and tomato slices, sprinkling half the herbs and half the mozzarella on top. Season with salt and pepper.

5. Layer in the remaining potato and tomato slices, and sprinkle with the rest of the herbs and salt and pepper.

6. Top with the rest of the onions and drizzle the remaining oil over the top. Sprinkle with the remaining cheese.

7. Cover with foil and bake in a 375°F (190°C) oven for about 30 minutes. Remove foil, and continue cooking for about 20 minutes longer, until potatoes are tender and the top is lightly browned.

Serves 4–6.

Hash-Brown Pancake

1½ lbs	potatoes	750 g
	salt and freshly ground pepper	
4 tbsp	oil *or* half oil, half butter	60 ml
1	small onion, *chopped*	
	fresh parsley, *chopped* (optional)	

TIPS:

• Boil up some extra potatoes when you're making potato salad, then use them for home fries or hash browns the next morning.

• Steps 1–3 can be done the day before.

A wedge of crispy potato pancake is the perfect accompaniment to eggs and sausages, or the fish you just caught.

1. Cover potatoes with cold, salted water, bring to a boil, and cook about 30 minutes until just tender. Drain at once and refrigerate until needed.

2. Peel skins from cold potatoes and grate, dice, or put them through a ricer.

3. Lightly cook onion in a little oil and add to potatoes. Season mixture with salt and pepper, and add parsley if you like.

4. Heat 2 tbsp (30 ml) of the oil in a large, non-stick frying pan. When the fat is hot – enough heat is critical – add the potatoes and press down to make an even layer. Cook for a few minutes, then loosen the underside of the potatoes and shake pan gently to be sure things aren't sticking. Cook for about 5 minutes until the underside is nicely browned.

5. Cover frying pan with a plate and invert the pancake onto the plate. Add a spoonful more oil to the pan and when it is hot, slide the cake back in, unbrowned side down. Cook until underside is browned and pancake is crisp, about 5 minutes more.

Serves 4.

IV. MAKE-AHEAD MAIN DISHES, PASTAS, & ONE-POT MEALS

SUMMER WEEKEND COOKBOOK

CROWD PLEASERS:

INVITE FRIENDS TO A CHILI CHALLENGE

Have each family bring a pot of their favourite chili, so everyone gets to try a number of different types. (The two chili recipes in this section provide a good starting point.) Part of the fun of eating chili is adding an assortment of toppings. Put out bowls of:

grated Monterey Jack or medium Cheddar cheese

sour cream, either plain or whipped with a squeeze of lime and fresh chopped coriander

chopped jalapeño peppers, either fresh or canned

chopped green or sweet onions

warm red kidney or pinto beans (if they're not included in the chilis)

Serve with baskets of warm corn bread (p. 199), tortillas, and crusty sourdough bread.

HAVE A POTLUCK SUPPER

Keep these dishes in mind when you're holding or going to a potluck supper. They're hearty, make a lot, and can be prepared in advance, then reheated in the oven or on top of the stove. Just add a big green salad and some fresh, crusty bread.

TOPPING IT OFF

Savoury main dish pies – such as beef or chicken pot pies – are great to set before a hungry group. If you find pastry topping too finicky and time-consuming, try one of these alternatives with your favourite filling:

Baking Powder Biscuits
(p. 201 for dough, p. 139 for method)

Corn Bread Topping *(p. 135)*

Mashed Potatoes with Herbs

Seasoned Bread Crumbs

Sweet & Spicy Sweet Potato Topping
(p. 135),
or a mixture of sweet potatoes
and carrots

(And if you want to stick with a pastry topping, you'll find the recipe on p. 215.)

Chicken & Sausage Jambalaya

2 tbsp	vegetable oil	30 ml
1 cup	smoked ham, *diced*	250 ml
½ cup	spicy smoked sausage, *diced*	125 ml
2 cups	boneless chicken breast, *diced*	500 ml
2	large onions, *finely chopped*	
4	celery stalks, *chopped*	
1	green pepper, *chopped*	
4 cloves	garlic, *finely chopped*	
2	bay leaves	
1 tsp	each oregano, cayenne, freshly ground pepper, and salt	5 ml
½ tsp	thyme	2 ml
1 tsp	filé *(optional)*	5 ml
2 cups	long-grain converted rice	500 ml
1 cup	tomatoes *(fresh or canned), chopped*	250 ml
3 cups	chicken stock	750 ml

A great one-pot dish originating in Louisiana kitchens. While sometimes difficult to find, filé (powdered sassafras leaves, sold in jars) is often used in Cajun cuisine to flavour and thicken soups and stews. The dish will be just fine, however, if you leave it out.

1. Heat oil in a large heavy pot, add ham and sausage, and brown lightly. Lift out and set aside.

2. Add chicken pieces and brown, then remove and set aside.

3. Add half of the onions, celery, and peppers to the pot, cooking until soft and well browned. Toss in the rest of the vegetables and the garlic, and cook over moderate heat until softened.

4. Return meats to pot with all the seasonings and cook for 5 minutes. Add rice and stir for a few minutes before adding tomatoes and stock. Bring mixture to a boil, lower heat, cover pot, and leave to cook gently for 20–25 minutes more until liquid is absorbed and rice is tender yet still has texture. Toss gently, remove from heat, cover, and leave to rest for 5 minutes. Serve hot.

Serves 6.

TIPS:

• If you want to prepare part of the Jambalaya ahead of time, cook the meats and vegetables as described above and add the tomatoes and stock, but do not add the rice. Refrigerate or freeze. When you are ready to serve, bring the mixture to a boil, add rice, and cook for 20–25 minutes as described above.

• Jambalaya often includes seafood, such as shrimp and/or fresh oysters; add them during the last 5 minutes of cooking. Add some hot sauce if you like things spicier.

Both Jambalaya (this page) and Chicken & Black-Eyed Peas (p. 130) are complete meals in a dish. Just add a green salad and some fresh crusty bread.

Chicken & Black-Eyed Peas

2 cans	black-eyed peas *(19 oz/540 ml)* or	
4 cups	cooked black-eyed peas *(see p. 110)*	1 L
12–16	chicken legs and thighs, *skin removed*	
2 tbsp	olive oil	30 ml
1–2 tsp	cumin seed	5–10 ml
2	large onions, *chopped*	
4 cloves	garlic, *finely chopped*	
1	green pepper, *chopped*	
2–3	fresh jalapeño peppers, *chopped*	
1 can	plum tomatoes, *drained (reserve juice) and chopped (28 oz/796 ml)*	
1 can	tomato paste *(5½ oz/156 ml)*	
1	bay leaf	
1 tsp	each basil and oregano	5 ml
¼ cup	parsley, *chopped*	60 ml
	salt and freshly ground pepper	
1 cup	mild Cheddar cheese, *grated*	250 ml

This hearty main course of chicken simmered in a rich sauce, then baked with black-eyed peas, has a satisfying warmth on a cool day.

1. Season chicken pieces with salt and pepper. Heat oil in a large, heavy skillet. Add 1 tsp (5 ml) cumin seed and heat until it pops. Brown chicken on all sides, in batches if necessary. (Heat another teaspoon of cumin seed in the oil before adding the second batch of chicken.) Remove and set aside.

2. In the same pan, brown the onion. Add garlic, green pepper, and jalapeños, and cook for a few minutes.

3. Transfer to a large pot and stir in chopped tomatoes and reserved juice, tomato paste, herbs, and seasonings. Bring sauce to a boil, then lower heat and return chicken pieces to the sauce; cover the pot, and leave to simmer until chicken is almost tender – about 30 minutes. Season to taste.

4. Remove the chicken from the sauce; toss the black-eyed peas with half the sauce and spread in two 8" x 8" (2-L) ovenproof casseroles. Arrange the chicken pieces on top of the peas and cover with the rest of the sauce. Cover the dishes with foil and set in a 350°F (180°C) oven. After about 20 minutes, remove foil and sprinkle with Cheddar cheese. Continue baking, uncovered, until cheese has melted and browned slightly (about 15 minutes longer).

Serves 6–8.

TIP:
• This dish can be assembled and then frozen (without cheese) before baking. When ready to serve, defrost in refrigerator, then bake for about 30 minutes before topping with cheese and proceeding as above.

(The Chicken &Black-Eyed Peas is shown in the photo on the previous page.)

Picadillo

2 tbsp	oil	30 ml
2	onions, *chopped*	
2 cloves	garlic, *minced*	
1	green pepper, *seeded and chopped*	
2 tbsp	jalapeño peppers *(or to taste), chopped*	30 ml
1½ lbs	ground beef	750 g
3	tomatoes *(fresh or canned), peeled and chopped*	
1 tbsp	tomato paste	15 ml
½ cup	water *or* stock	125 ml
1 tsp	oregano	5 ml
	salt and freshly ground pepper	
½ cup	raisins *(optional)*	125 ml
½ cup	slivered almonds *(optional)*	125 ml
¼ cup	pimiento-stuffed green olives, *sliced (optional)*	60 ml

Picadillo, which means "minced meat" in Spanish, is a wonderful spicy mixture of Latin American origins that is traditionally served over rice. This dish is very popular with the younger set, and when turned into a taco feast, it's a great way to feed a teenage group of indeterminate number and unpredictable (though usually huge) appetite. Set out the picadillo accompanied by baskets of warm taco shells, lots of toppings – shredded lettuce, grated Cheddar cheese, extra chopped fresh tomato and onion, sour cream, and salsa – and piles of napkins.

1. In a large, heavy pan, sauté onion and garlic in oil until soft. Add sweet and hot peppers and cook briefly.

2. Add ground beef and brown. Stir in tomatoes, tomato paste, water or stock, oregano, and a dash of salt and pepper.

3. Simmer about 20 minutes. Stir in raisins, almonds, and olives and heat through. Taste and adjust seasoning.

Serves 4.

TIPS:

• The picadillo can be made ahead. Cool, cover, and refrigerate or freeze until needed.

• The recipe multiplies easily to feed a gang.

Quick Curry

1	**medium onion**	
2" piece	**fresh ginger,** *peeled and roughly chopped*	5 cm
4–6 cloves	**garlic,** *finely chopped*	
2 tbsp	**vegetable oil**	30 ml
2–3 tsp	**curry powder**	10–15 ml
½ tsp	**cayenne** *(optional)*	2 ml
1½ lbs	**ground beef** *or* **ground lamb**	750 g
2	**tomatoes,** *chopped,* **or**	
1 cup	**canned tomatoes,** *drained and chopped*	250 ml
¼ cup	**yoghurt**	60 ml
	salt	
1 cup	**fresh or frozen peas**	250 ml

Garnish

1 tsp	**cumin seeds,** *toasted*	5 ml
1	**hot green chile,** *seeded and chopped*	
1 tbsp	**fresh coriander,** *chopped (optional)*	15 ml

In authentic curry recipes, the sauce includes a long list of spices, which traditional cooks meticulously roast and grind together. This recipe simplifies and shortens the process by using prepared curry powder and just a couple of other easy-to-find spices and flavourings. An added bonus is that curries are meant to be prepared ahead – they taste better after they have been sitting in the refrigerator for a day. This recipe also freezes well. Serve with rice, chutney, raita (see Quick Tricks, p. 72) and pita bread (or Indian breads, if available).

1. Combine onion, ginger, and garlic in a blender or food processor and process briefly to make a paste. (Or chop finely by hand.)

2. Heat oil in a large skillet and stir-fry onion mixture quickly until browned. Sprinkle with curry powder and cayenne, then add meat, breaking up the lumps; cook for a few minutes until nicely browned.

3. Stir in tomatoes, salt lightly, and simmer for about 20 minutes. Stir in yoghurt. If the mixture seems dry, add a little water (or stock) as it simmers.

4. Add peas and cook for about 5 minutes longer. Garnish with cumin, chile, and coriander, and serve over rice.

Serves 4–6.

TIP:

• Instead of the ground meat, substitute cubed beef or lamb, or even bone-in chicken pieces. (Increase the quantity of the chicken to about 3 lbs/1.5 kg.) First, brown the meat in the oil. Set aside, and proceed with the recipe as above, returning the meat to the pan with the curry powder and adding about 1 cup (250 ml) of stock or water. Increase the simmering time to about 1½ hours, or until the meat is tender.

Curries make excellent food for a casual party. Shown here: Quick Curry on rice, with cooling cucumber-yoghurt raita and onion relish.

Creole Chicken Pie

2 tbsp	olive oil	30 ml
2 lbs	**boneless chicken,** *cut in 1½" (3-cm) pieces*	1 kg
3	**medium onions,** *chopped*	
4 cloves	**garlic,** *finely chopped*	
1	**red pepper,** *chopped*	
1	**green pepper,** *chopped*	
1 tsp	paprika	5 ml
½ tsp	cayenne	2 ml
1 tbsp	flour	15 ml
1 can	**plum tomatoes,** *drained and chopped (28 oz/796 ml)*	
1 cup	chicken stock	250 ml
1 tsp	thyme	5 ml
1 tsp	oregano	5 ml
	salt and freshly ground pepper	
	Corn Bread Topping *or* **Sweet & Spicy Sweet Potato Topping**	

This southern-style pie can have a traditional pastry crust (p. 215), but it's also delicious with a topping of spicy sweet potatoes or corn bread. If time is really limited, the chicken filling can be heated alone and served with a side dish of long-grain rice.

1. Heat oil in a large saucepan. Add chicken pieces in batches and brown lightly on all sides – about 10 minutes. Remove and set aside.

2. Add onions and cook until soft. Add garlic and peppers and cook for 5 minutes. Stir in paprika, cayenne, and flour, and continue to stir over medium heat for a minute or two. Add tomatoes, stock, herbs, and seasonings. Simmer for about 20 minutes.

3. Return chicken pieces to the pot, simmer for 5 minutes, taste, and adjust seasoning. Spoon filling into a shallow 4–6 cup (1–1.5 L) casserole dish.

4. At this point, the mixture may be covered and stored overnight in the refrigerator or for several weeks in the freezer. When you want to serve, finish the pie with one of the toppings on the facing page.

Serves 4–6.

TIPS:

•If the filling has been in the freezer, set it in the refrigerator overnight to thaw before proceeding with topping.

• A mixture of light and dark chicken meat will give more flavour to the dish. Put dark meat in first, as it takes a little longer to cook than the breast meat.

Corn Bread Topping

¾ cup	yellow corn meal	175 ml
½ cup	flour	125 ml
1 tbsp	sugar	15 ml
1½ tsp	baking powder	7 ml
½ tsp	salt	2 ml
¾ cup	milk	175 ml
⅓ cup	melted butter, *cooled*	75 ml
1	**egg,** *lightly beaten*	

Sweet & Spicy Sweet Potato Topping

4	sweet potatoes	
2 tbsp	butter	30 ml
1 tsp	brown sugar	5 ml
½ tsp	ground ginger	2 ml
½ tsp	cinnamon	2 ml
pinch	salt	
dash	lemon juice	
	coarsely ground black pepper	

Corn Bread Topping

1. If the chicken filling has been in the refrigerator, cover casserole and heat in 375°F (190°C) oven for 15–20 minutes.

2. While chicken is heating, prepare topping: Combine dry ingredients. Beat together milk, butter, and egg. Stir liquid into corn meal mixture.

3. Spoon over chicken in casserole. Bake an additional 25–30 minutes until filling is bubbling and top is cooked and lightly browned. Serve hot.

Sweet & Spicy Sweet Potato Topping

1. Bake sweet potatoes at 400°F (200°C) for about 30 minutes until just tender (or peel, cut into pieces, and boil in lightly salted water for 15 minutes). Remove skins. Mash until smooth, then beat in butter and seasonings.

2. Spread in an even layer over prepared chicken casserole and sprinkle with black pepper. Dot with butter if desired. Bake at 350°F (180°C) for about 30–40 minutes until chicken is bubbling and topping is lightly browned.

Spaghetti alla Puttanesca

¼ cup	**olive oil**	**60 ml**
4 cloves	**garlic,** *finely chopped*	
1 can	**anchovy fillets,** *chopped (2 oz/50 g)*	
1 can	**plum tomatoes,** *drained (reserve juice) and chopped (28 oz/796 ml)*	
pinch	**dried red chile flakes** *(optional)*	
¼ cup	**capers,** *drained*	**60 ml**
½ cup	**black olives,** *pitted and chopped*	**125 ml**
	fresh parsley, *chopped*	
	freshly ground pepper	
1 lb	**spaghetti**	**500 g**

This robustly flavoured dish is quickly and easily put together. The story goes that it was named for the puttane, the "ladies of the night" who had little time for shopping or fancy footwork in the kitchen! As its name implies, this dish has earthy "adult" flavours and may not be enjoyed by those with inexperienced taste buds.

1. Cook garlic and anchovies in oil for a few minutes until softened.

2. Add tomatoes and juice, and the chile flakes, if desired. Simmer 10 minutes.

3. Add capers and olives and simmer about 10–15 minutes longer, until sauce is nicely thickened.

4. Cook spaghetti until *al dente* (tender, yet still somewhat firm) and drain well. Toss sauce with hot pasta in a warm bowl. Taste, adjust seasoning, and serve at once.

Serves 4.

TIPS:

• A large cooking pot is essential to preparing good pasta. In a small pot, the water cannot circulate around the pasta, which consequently cooks unevenly and sticks together. Each 4 oz (125 g) of pasta requires 1 qt (1 L) of boiling water and at least ¼ tsp (1 ml) of salt.

• With good-quality pasta, it's not necessary to add oil to the water to keep the pasta from sticking.

• If anchovies straight from the can have too dominant a flavour for your taste, simply rinse them under cold water and pat dry before using.

Clockwise from left: Spaghetti alla Puttanesca (this page), crumb-topped Penne with Mixed Cheeses (p.138), and super-quick Black Olive Pasta (p. 140).

Penne with Mixed Cheeses

1½–2 cups	cheese, *grated*	375–500 ml
¼ cup	**Parmesan**, *grated*	60 ml
1½ tbsp	**flour**	20 ml
¼ cup	**butter**	60 ml
1 cup	**milk** *or* **cream**	250 ml
pinch	**ground nutmeg**	
	salt *(if necessary)*	
1 lb	**penne** *(or other favourite pasta shape)*	500 g
1 cup	**seasoned breadcrumbs** *(optional, for topping)*	250 ml

TIPS:

• Finely grate hard cheeses such as Parmesan and aged Cheddar. Softer cheeses – Fontina, medium Cheddar, and mozzarella – can be roughly grated or cut into small pieces.

• Add the harder cheeses first, because they take longer to melt; stir in the soft cheeses just before serving.

This version of that old family favourite, macaroni-and-cheese, is an easy substitute when you've run out of the stand-by packaged version – and I guarantee the family will like it better! You can use up odds and ends of various cheeses, as long as the flavours blend.

1. Toss the cheese together with the flour. Set aside.

2. In a large, heavy pan heat butter and milk or cream. Sprinkle in cheese, a small handful at a time, adding the softer cheese just at the end. Stir mixture continuously over gentle heat until it forms a smooth sauce between each addition of cheese. Add seasonings.

3. Meanwhile, cook the pasta in a large quantity of boiling, salted water. Drain thoroughly and combine with the cheese sauce. Either serve at once with a garnish of fresh pepper and chopped parsley or, if you like a crispy topping, transfer the pasta and cheese sauce to a shallow buttered casserole dish. Sprinkle with seasoned breadcrumbs and a little more grated cheese. Dot with butter and set under the broiler for a few minutes.

Serves 4.

TIP:

• When making any cheese sauce, use a low temperature – too high a heat and your sauce will become grainy.

(Penne with Mixed Cheeses is shown in the photo on the previous page.)

Beef Braised in Beer over Egg Noodles

3–4 tbsp	vegetable oil	45–60 ml
3 lbs	lean stewing beef, *trimmed and cut into cubes*	1.5 kg
½ lb	small mushrooms, *cleaned and trimmed*	250 g
6	medium onions, *sliced*	
4 cloves	garlic, *minced*	
3 tbsp	flour	45 ml
	salt and freshly ground pepper	
2 cups	beef stock *or* beef bouillon	500 ml
2 cups	dark ale	500 ml
1 tbsp	brown sugar	15 ml
1 tbsp	red wine vinegar	15 ml
1 tsp	thyme	5 ml
2	bay leaves	
1 lb	carrots, *quartered lengthwise and cut into pieces*	500 g
1½ lbs	egg noodles	750 g

This stew is wonderful served over broad egg noodles, which soak up the delicious gravy. Make it a day ahead to allow the flavour to develop; return it to a simmer and cook the noodles just before serving.

1. Heat 2 tbsp (30 ml) oil in a large, heavy pot. Pat beef cubes dry and brown well, in batches. As the meat browns, remove it to a side dish.

2. In the same pot, adding a little more oil if needed, lightly brown mushrooms. Season and set aside. Add onions to pot and lightly brown. Stir in garlic and cook for a few minutes.

3. Return meat to pot, sprinkle with flour, season lightly, and toss over high heat for a couple of minutes. Stir in stock, ale, brown sugar, vinegar, and herbs. Gently bring to a boil, stirring constantly. Lower the heat and cover.

4. Simmer over very low heat or braise in a 325°F (160°C) oven until the meat is tender, about 2 hours. After 1 hour, add carrots. Stir in mushrooms when meat is tender. Taste and adjust seasoning.

5. When ready to serve, cook noodles according to package directions. Serve stew over noodles.

Serves 6.

TIP:

•Instead of serving the stew over noodles, top with Baking Powder Biscuits (p. 201). Make the biscuit dough, omitting the ham. Shortly before serving, gently reheat the stew and turn it into a shallow ovenproof casserole. Drop mounds of dough on top of the hot stew and bake, uncovered, in a 375°F (190°C) oven for about 15 minutes until biscuits are nicely browned.

Three Super-Quick Sauces

These easy-to-prepare pasta sauces taste as though you slaved over them for hours. Each recipe makes enough sauce for 1 lb (500 g) of dried pasta.

Seafood Sauce

In a saucepan, combine 3 cups (750 ml) tomato sauce, a squeeze of fresh orange juice, a few shakes of hot sauce, and ¹/₂ cup (125 ml) heavy cream. Heat to simmering. Drain 2 cans (7 oz/198 g) of tuna, crab, shrimp, or lobster and add to the sauce, breaking the seafood up with a fork. Heat through, season to taste, and serve over hot, drained pasta with a sprinkling of parsley.

Red Pepper Pasta

Cook 2 finely chopped cloves of garlic in 2 tbsp (30 ml) hot olive oil until soft. Drain a small jar of pimientos and chop roughly. Add to pan and heat through. Toss with hot, drained pasta in a warm bowl and sprinkle with fresh chopped parsley and freshly ground black pepper.

Black Olive Pasta

Toss hot, drained pasta in a warm bowl with 2 tbsp (30 ml) olive oil, 4 tbsp (60 ml) tapenade (black olive paste, sold in jars), and finely chopped fresh parsley. Serve at once.

TIP:
• Pasta is best when it is served steaming hot, straight from the pot. Have everyone seated at the table, enjoying hot bruschetta (p. 38) or garlic bread, ready and waiting as the pasta dish is completed.

Baked Beans Beyond Belief

6 strips	**bacon,** *cut in 2" (5-cm) pieces*	
1	**large red onion,** *very thinly sliced*	
2 cans	**dark brown beans** *(19 oz/540 ml apiece)*	
2 tbsp	**coffee,** *finely ground (or more if you like)*	**30 ml**
1 tsp	**dry mustard**	**5 ml**
½ cup	**maple syrup**	**125 ml**

This is a maple-flavoured version of a favourite old cottage and camp stand-by. It's excellent with baked ham or grilled country sausages, and slabs of whole-wheat toast. Don't skimp on the freshly ground coffee; it may sound like an unusual ingredient, but it adds a wonderful depth of flavour to the dish.

1. In a large frying pan, cook bacon pieces over moderate heat until lightly browned. Remove and set aside.

2. In the same pan, cook onion until soft.

3. Line the bottom of an 8-cup (2-L) casserole with half the bacon. Cover with a thin layer of onions, then spread about a 1" (2-cm) layer of the beans on top. Repeat the onion and bean layering twice more.

4. Sprinkle finely ground coffee on top. Stir mustard into maple syrup to dissolve, and pour all over. Top with remaining bacon.

5. Cover and bake in a 350°F (180°C) oven for 30 minutes. Remove cover and continue to bake about 15 minutes longer until beans are bubbling and have thickened nicely.

Serves 4–6.

Tex-Mex Chili

10	dried ancho chiles	
4	dried chipotle chiles	
2–4	jalapeño peppers, *fresh or canned*	
4 tbsp	lard, bacon fat, *or* **oil**	60 ml
4	medium onions, *chopped*	
2 tbsp	garlic, *finely chopped*	30 ml
3 lbs	stewing beef, *finely chopped*	1.5 kg
1 tbsp	each paprika and cumin	15 ml
1 tsp	each dried oregano and basil	5 ml
2 cups	plum tomatoes *(fresh or canned),* *peeled, seeded, and* *chopped*	500 ml
2–4 cups	beef stock *or* **water**	500 ml–1 L
	salt and freshly ground pepper	
3 cups	cooked red kidney beans *or* pinto beans, *drained*	750 ml

No two chili devotees agree on what makes a great chili. This version gets its rich, wonderful taste from a purée of dried chiles rather than chile powder. And it starts with chunks of beef rather than ground beef – traditional chili cooks finely chop or coarsely grind the beef themselves. True Texas-style chili does not contain beans, so if you want to be a purist, leave them out or serve them on the side.

1. Prepare a purée from the dried chiles as described on p. 14. Broil, peel, seed, and chop the fresh jalapeños, or rinse and chop the canned ones. Set the chiles aside.

2. In a heavy skillet, heat 2 tbsp (30 ml) of the fat over medium heat. Add onions and cook until soft, stir in garlic, and cook for a few minutes.

3. In a large, heavy pot, heat the remaining fat. Add the chopped beef and brown lightly (in several batches if necessary). Add the onions and garlic, the chile purée, and the spices, and toss briefly over the heat. Stir in the tomatoes and stock, and season to taste. Bring to a boil, lower heat, and simmer, partially covered, for 1^1/$_2$–2 hours, stirring occasionally.

4. Before serving, taste and adjust seasoning; stir in jalapeños and beans, or simply serve them alongside.

Serves 6–8.

TIPS:

• For a different flavour, replace part of the beef with pork.

• Make a big batch, since leftover chili freezes well.

Black Bean & Vegetable Chili

3 tbsp	vegetable oil	45 ml
1	large onion, *chopped*	
4 cloves	garlic, *finely chopped*	
1	red pepper, *seeded and chopped*	
1	green pepper, *seeded and chopped*	
1–2	jalapeño peppers, *seeded and chopped*	
1 tbsp	dried oregano	15 ml
1 tbsp	cumin	15 ml
½–1 tsp	cayenne	2–5 ml
1–2 tbsp	chile powder	15–30 ml
	salt and freshly ground pepper	
1 can	plum tomatoes *chopped, with juice* (28 oz/796 ml)	
½ cup	bulgur *(optional)*	125 ml
2 cans	black beans, *drained and rinsed* (19 oz/540 ml) **or**	
4 cups	cooked black beans *(cooking instructions on p. 110; reserve cooking liquid)*	1 L

Serve this spicy chili accompanied with bowls of grated cheese, additional chopped roasted hot chiles, sour cream, chopped green onions, chopped coriander, and warm corn bread (p. 199) or tortillas. Include other vegetables in the chili if you like – cubes of squash or pumpkin (blanch them first until almost tender), carrots, celery, green beans, and potatoes.

1. Heat oil over medium heat in a large, heavy pot. Add onion and cook for 5 minutes. Stir in garlic, vegetables, and spices, and toss over medium heat for 5 more minutes.

2. Add tomatoes, juice, and bulgur (optional), and gently simmer, covered, for 30 minutes.

3. Add beans and about 1 cup (250 ml) of water (or cooking liquid, if you prepared your own beans). Continue simmering, uncovered, until chili is nicely thickened and well flavoured, about 30 minutes longer.

Serves 6.

TIPS:

• The bulgur (available in bulk-food stores and some supermarkets) makes this a more complete main dish, but the chili is still delicious without it.

• If you've got some dry sherry on hand, add a splash or two when you add the beans.

V. SOUPS & SANDWICHES

Bread doesn't just come in loaves.
Make sandwiches more interesting by
building them on a variety of bases.
Here are some possibilities:

a baguette, cut into thick slices

pita bread pockets

bagels

crusty buns

focaccia

tortillas, for rolling around
various fillings

Middle Eastern flatbread
(Azim is one popular brand)

Other great things to stuff in pita pockets for lunch

*You'll find these recipes in Section III,
Salads & Side Dishes:*

CROWD PLEASERS:

A DO-IT-YOURSELF SANDWICH SPREAD

A midday meal can be difficult to plan when you've got a bunch of guests who go off for different activities in the morning and don't necessarily get together at the same instant for lunch. To make life easy for the cook, set out a casual do-it-yourself sandwich buffet: cold cuts, cheeses, condiments, breads, and fresh fruits. Make it out-of-the-ordinary by including a variety of interesting breads and condiments – maybe a fresh salsa (such as Pico de Gallo, p. 111), a jar of chutney, or an herb butter in addition to mayo and Dijon-style mustard. And don't forget the pickles: crispy dills, along with some hot pepper rings for the spicy-food fans.

OTHER COMBOS TO TRY

You'll find recipes for these sandwich components throughout the book.

Thinly sliced Texas Barbecued Brisket (p. 44)
piled on warm grilled slices of baguette and slathered with
Tangy Texas Barbecue Sauce (p. 45)

•

Sliced Chile-Rub Chicken (p. 63)
or
Spicy Shredded Chicken (p.151)
topped with avocado slices and salsa and rolled in a tortilla

•

Grilled Italian sausage stuffed in a crusty kaiser with
roasted hot and sweet peppers *(p. 90) and tomato sauce on top*

•

Slices of barbecued
Marinated Leg of Lamb *(Tip, p. 69) in a pita topped with*
Greek Salad *(p. 117) and* **tzatziki** *(Tips, p. 76).*

•

Grilled portobello mushrooms (p. 90)
on a focaccia topped with
roasted hot and sweet peppers *(p.90) and a slice of provolone or mozzarella*

Leek & Potato Soup *with Stilton*

4	**leeks,** *thinly sliced (white and tender green parts only)*	
3	**medium potatoes,** *peeled and diced*	
5 cups	**vegetable** *or* **chicken stock**	**(1.25 L)**
	salt and freshly ground pepper	
¼ cup	**35% cream**	**60 ml**
½ cup	**Stilton cheese,** *crumbled*	**125 ml**
	fresh chives *or* **parsley,** *chopped*	

Potatoes and leeks make a comforting combination that's open to all manner of variations. Just remember to add about equal amounts of liquid and chopped vegetables. Serve with Steak Sandwiches with Horseradish Cream (facing page).

1. Combine leeks, potatoes, stock, and about ¼ tsp (1 ml) of salt in a large pot. Bring to a boil, reduce heat, and simmer, partially covered, until vegetables are tender – about 40 minutes.

2. Purée mixture until smooth. Just before serving, stir in cream and Stilton, and heat through. Season to taste.

3. Garnish with fresh chives or parsley and a little extra crumbled cheese on top of each bowl if desired.

Serves 4–6.

TIPS:

• For a different taste, omit the cheese but include another ¼ cup (60 ml) of cream or a tablespoon or two (15–30 ml) of butter.

• Instead of puréeing the soup, serve it chunky style. Thicken it by puréeing just a cup or so of cooked vegetables and stock, then stir the purée back into the pot.

• Add a cup or so (250 ml) of broccoli or watercress, or 2 packed cups (500 ml) of fresh spinach, to the cooked potato/leek mixture. Simmer all together gently for 5 minutes. Purée if desired, then add a dash of grated nutmeg and the cream.

• To make a classic vichyssoise to serve cold, purée the cooked potato/leek mixture and press through a sieve to make a smooth cream. Stir in ½ cup (125 ml) 35% cream and chill. Season to taste. Serve garnished with chopped fresh chives.

Steak Sandwich with Horseradish Cream

1½ lbs	**rare roast beef** *or* **steak,** *sliced thinly on the diagonal*	750 g
6 slices	**sourdough** *or* **French bread,** *about* ½" *(1 cm) thick*	
	Horseradish Cream	
1 bunch	**fresh watercress** *or* **romaine lettuce**	
2	**Grilled Red Onions** *(recipe on p.88)*	
	salt and freshly ground pepper	

Horseradish Cream

½ cup	**mayonnaise**	125 ml
½ cup	**sour cream**	125 ml
1 tbsp	**prepared horseradish,** *well drained*	15 ml

This open-faced sandwich is a treat when you are lucky enough to have leftover roast beef or grilled steak. It's great with grilled red onions, or substitute a slice of dill pickle if you like.

1. Combine ingredients for the Horseradish Cream.

2. Lightly toast the bread slices. Spread each slice with Horseradish Cream and add layers of watercress or lettuce and sliced roast beef or steak.

3. Top with grilled onions and season with salt and pepper.

Serves 6.

 QUICK TRICK:

The world's best (and easiest) summer sandwich: toasted whole-grain bread, mayo, fat slices of ripe tomato, a few torn-up fresh basil leaves, and ground pepper. Add a few crispy bacon slices and fresh leaf lettuce if you like. Perfection.

Sweet Potato & Chile Soup

2 tbsp	**unsalted butter**	30 ml
2	**medium onions,** *finely chopped*	
2	**cloves garlic,** *finely chopped*	
3	**medium sweet potatoes,** *peeled and sliced*	
1	**jalapeño pepper** *(or more to taste), seeded and chopped*	
1 tsp	**chipotle** *or* **other chile purée** *(optional; see p. 14)*	5 ml
4–5 cups	**chicken** *or* **vegetable stock**	1–1.25 L
	salt	
	juice of 2 limes *(about ¼ cup/60 ml), or to taste*	
	sour cream *or* **yoghurt**	

The sweetness of the potatoes, the heat of the chiles, and the tartness of the lime create a wonderfully complex flavour. Serve with Chicken Quesadillas (p. 150).

1. Heat butter in a large pot. Add onions and soften over medium heat. Add garlic, sweet potatoes, jalapeño pepper, and chile purée (optional), and stir to coat with the buttery onions.

2. Add 4 cups (1 L) chicken stock and a dash of salt. Bring to a boil, reduce heat, and simmer, partially covered, until the vegetables are tender – about 20 minutes. Purée the mixture.

3. Reheat gently, add lime juice, and season to taste. The soup will thicken as it rests, so adjust consistency with additional stock as needed.

4. Serve hot with a swirl of sour cream or yoghurt in each bowl.

Serves 6.

TIPS:

• This soup is even better when made a day or two ahead, so that flavours have a chance to blend. It also freezes well.

• For a great informal dinner that can be completely made ahead, serve the Sweet Potato & Chile Soup and Chicken Quesadillas with a Corn & Black Bean Salsa (p. 110).

Clockwise from front: Sweet Potato & Chile Soup (this page), Chicken Quesadillas (next page), Red Clam Chowder (p. 159), and Broccoli Soup (Tips, p. 146).

Chicken Quesadillas

6   **large flour tortillas**
(10"/25 cm)

1 cup   **red** *or* **green salsa**   **250 ml**

½ lb   **Monterey Jack** *or*   **250 g**
mild Cheddar cheese,
grated

jalapeño peppers,
chopped (optional)

Spicy Shredded Chicken
(recipe on facing page)

fresh coriander *or*
parsley, *chopped*

These tortillas, stacked with layers of tasty fillings, make great party food and are easy to serve since they can be assembled ahead of time and heated in the oven when needed.

1. Place two tortillas on a lightly oiled baking sheet. Spread each with a tablespoon or two of salsa and a layer of grated cheese, chopped jalapeños if desired, and shredded chicken.

2. Top with another tortilla and repeat the layers of salsa, cheese, jalapeños, and chicken. Add another tortilla, then spread more salsa and cheese on top.

3. Bake in 350°F (180°C) oven for about 15 minutes until the quesadillas are hot and the cheese is melted.

4. Serve hot, cut in wedges and sprinkled with coriander or parsley.

Serves 6.

TIPS:

• Steps 1 and 2 can be done a few hours ahead. Refrigerate until serving time.

• If you don't have time to make the Spicy Shredded Chicken, try shredded smoked chicken (sold in food shops and delicatessens) in the quesadillas instead – delicious!

(The Chicken Quesadillas are shown in the photo on the previous page.)

Spicy Shredded Chicken

1 tsp	cumin	5 ml
¼ tsp	cayenne	1 ml
1 tsp	dried thyme	5 ml
2	**cloves garlic,** *finely chopped*	
2 tbsp	**onion,** *chopped*	30 ml
4	**boneless, skinless chicken breasts**	
2 tbsp	oil	30 ml
½ cup	**beer, white wine,** *or* **chicken stock**	125 ml
	salt	

Use this recipe for the Chicken Quesadillas on the facing page, or roll the strips in a tortilla, along with avocado slices and salsa.

1. Combine cumin, cayenne, thyme, garlic, and onion, and mash together to make a paste. Cut chicken breasts lengthwise into strips and coat with mixture. Leave to marinate at room temperature for 30 minutes (or longer in the refrigerator).

2. Heat oil in a large skillet. Add chicken and cook briefly over moderately high heat.

3. Add beer, wine, or stock, cover pan, and cook gently until chicken is cooked through and nicely glazed – about 5 minutes. Taste and season.

4. Shred chicken strips into convenient bite-sized lengths when ready to assemble the tortillas.

Makes 3 cups (750 ml).

TIP:
• The chicken can be prepared the day before and refrigerated until needed.

Grilled Tomato-Basil Soup

2 lbs	**ripe tomatoes,** *halved*	1 kg
	olive oil	
	salt and freshly ground pepper	
1	**medium onion,** *peeled and quartered*	
1	**carrot,** *chopped*	
1 clove	**garlic,** *minced*	
3–4 cups	**chicken** *or* **vegetable stock**	750 ml–1 L
	flavourings tied together: *celery tops, thyme, parsley sprigs, and a bay leaf*	
¼ cup	**fresh basil,** *chopped*	60 ml
	lemon juice	
pinch	**sugar**	
	yoghurt *(for garnish)*	

TIP:

• 1 medium tomato weighs about 6 oz (175 g).

Grilling the tomatoes and onion adds an interesting smoky flavour to the soup. Serve chilled, topped with a swirl of yoghurt and fresh herbs.

1. Rub tomatoes and onion with oil, salt, and pepper. Set on the grill over low heat for about 10 minutes until flesh is lightly charred, turning once.

2. Combine tomatoes, onion, carrot, garlic, 3 cups (750 ml) stock, flavourings, and a little salt in a large pot. Bring to a boil, lower heat, and simmer for about 30 minutes until vegetables are soft.

3. Remove and discard flavouring bundle. Purée vegetables in a blender or food processor until smooth. Or press the soup through a food mill or sieve to remove seeds and skins, if you like. Stir in the chopped basil.

4. Adjust flavour with lemon juice and perhaps a pinch or two of sugar. Add more stock if necessary to achieve the desired consistency. Season to taste.

5. Serve chilled (or hot, if you like) with a swirl of yoghurt in each bowl and a garnish of basil.

Serves 6.

TIPS:

• For a cream of tomato soup that's excellent both hot and chilled, heat 1 cup (250 ml) of 18% cream for a few minutes and add to the puréed vegetables in place of the additional stock.

• The soup can also be made without grilling the vegetables first. Just chop roughly before adding to the pot.

Served chilled with yoghurt, Grilled Tomato-Basil Soup is wonderful on a hot summer day.

Mini-Meatball-Stuffed Pitas

½ cup	fine bulgur	125 ml
2 tbsp	olive oil	30 ml
1	small onion, *finely chopped*	
1 lb	lean ground beef	500 g
2 tbsp	toasted pine nuts *(optional)*	30 ml
2 tbsp	fresh parsley *or* coriander, *chopped*	30 ml
2 tbsp	fresh mint, *chopped*	30 ml
	salt and freshly ground pepper	
6	pita breads	
	Gazpacho Salad *(recipe on p. 119)*	

These mini-meatballs were inspired by a picnic recipe from a Brazilian friend. Bake or grill them beforehand, then serve them cold, tucked into pitas and topped with Gazpacho Salad (p. 119). The meatballs are equally delicious served hot off the grill. If you're going on a picnic, transport the sandwich components separately and assemble them when it's time to eat.

1. Cover bulgur with cold water and soak for 30 minutes. Strain and squeeze dry.

2. Heat olive oil in a frying pan, add onion, and cook until soft.

3. Combine onion with soaked bulgur, ground beef, and remaining ingredients. Add a few tablespoons of water, if necessary, to make a smooth, light mixture.

4. Form the mixture into small balls. (You should have about 24.) Place on a baking sheet and bake at 375°F (190°C) for about 20 minutes until browned and cooked through. Or thread on skewers and grill on barbecue for about 15 minutes, turning occasionally.

5. When ready to serve, tuck 4 meatballs into each pita and top with Gazpacho Salad.

Makes 6 sandwiches.

TIPS:
• Bulgur is a type of cracked wheat that has a nutty flavour and a soft texture. It's available at bulk-food stores as well as many supermarkets.

African-Style Tomato Soup

2 tbsp	olive oil	30 ml
1	onion, *chopped*	
5 cloves	garlic, *minced*	
1 tsp	cumin	5 ml
½ tsp	cayenne	2 ml
1 tbsp	chili powder	15 ml
1 can	plum tomatoes (28 oz/796 ml)	
¼ cup	tomato paste	60 ml
2 cups	water	500 ml
1 cup	smooth peanut butter	250 ml
1 tsp	hot sauce	5 ml
2 tbsp	white vinegar	30 ml
2 tsp	sugar	10 ml
	salt and freshly ground pepper	
1	lemon	

TIP:

• Canned foods are frequently salty. When using them, don't add salt to a dish until you have tasted it.

This rich, spicy soup couldn't be easier: It takes barely 20 minutes to make and uses ingredients that are usually on hand in the kitchen cupboard. Although the combination of peanut butter and tomatoes may sound unusual, the result is delicious. If you're a real hot-food fan, add more cayenne and hot sauce.

1. Cook onion and garlic in oil until golden. Stir in spices and cook for a minute or so.

2. Crush tomatoes with your hand, breaking into small pieces. Add tomatoes and their liquid, tomato paste, and water to the onion mixture.

3. Bring to a simmer, then reduce heat to low and stir in peanut butter, hot sauce, vinegar, and sugar. Cook over low heat at a bare simmer for 10 minutes, stirring occasionally. (This soup burns easily, so don't let it come to a boil.)

4. Season to taste, adding a squeeze of lemon and a splash more hot sauce if you like. Serve hot with a lemon slice in each bowl.

Serves 6.

QUICK TRICK:

Canned soups can sometimes save the day, especially if you jazz them up. For an instant creamy clam chowder, lightly brown 2 slices of bacon cut into pieces; pour off the fat. Drain a can of clams, reserving the juice, and toss them into the pan; heat through. Add reserved clam juice, a can of cream of potato soup, and 1 cup (250 ml) of milk or cream. Season with thyme and freshly ground pepper, and simmer for 5 minutes.

Stash-and-Go Sandwich

Speedy Pizza Crust *(recipe on p. 190)*		
2	**eggs,** *beaten*	
2 cups	**Swiss cheese,** *shredded*	500 ml
1 cup	**salami,** *diced*	250 ml
1 cup	**kielbasa,** *diced*	250 ml
¼ cup	**fresh parsley,** *chopped*	60 ml
2 tbsp	**green pepper,** *sweet or hot, chopped*	30 ml
¼ tsp	**paprika**	1 ml
	freshly ground pepper	1 ml

Glaze

1	**egg**	
1 tbsp	**water**	15 ml
1 tbsp	**poppy seeds**	15 ml

Especially tasty warm from the oven, but also great to pack in a picnic lunch.

1. Prepare Speedy Pizza Crust through Step 4.

2. With oiled fingers, roll or press half the dough into a 12" (30-cm) circle on pizza pan or baking sheet.

3. Combine all ingredients for filling. Spread evenly over dough in pan. Roll or stretch remaining half of dough to same-size circle. Place over filling. Seal and flute edges. Prick top with fork. Cover lightly with foil.

4. Bake at 400°F (200°C) for 45 minutes. Remove foil.

5. Beat egg and water together for glaze. Brush over crust. Sprinkle with poppy seeds. Bake uncovered 10–15 minutes, or until golden brown. Cut into wedges to serve.

Makes about 8 servings.

TIPS:

• To store, cool completely, then wrap well and refrigerate for up to 2 days, or freeze.

• Adjust the filling to take advantage of what you have on hand; try other cheeses such as Cheddar or mozzarella, and meats such as cooked chicken or ham. Sesame seeds sprinkled on top would also be nice.

• Make a vegetarian version by substituting 2 cups (500 ml) of chopped roasted vegetables (recipe on p. 90) for the salami and kielbasa.

MM COOKBOOK

Classic Gazpacho

1–2 cloves	**garlic,** *crushed*	
1 tsp	**salt**	5 ml
1 slice	**white bread,** *crusts removed*	
2 tbsp	**olive oil**	30 ml
2 cans	**plum tomatoes,** *drained and chopped; liquid reserved)* *(28 oz/796 ml)*	
½	**onion,** *chopped*	
2	**English cucumbers,** *peeled and chopped*	
2	**sweet green peppers** *(or mix green and red), seeded and chopped*	
¼ cup	**red wine vinegar**	60 ml
dash	**hot sauce** *(or to taste)*	
	salt and freshly ground pepper	
	croutons, sour cream, green onions, *chopped (for garnish)*	

A refreshing summer soup that can easily be assembled ahead of time at home with a blender or food processor. Serve with toasted ham-and-cheese sandwiches for a quick lunch or evening snack.

1. Crush garlic with salt in a large bowl. Add bread and oil and leave for 30 minutes.

2. In batches, blend or finely chop vegetables in a blender or food processor. Mix with bread in bowl, adding vinegar and seasonings. Adjust consistency with the reserved liquid from the tomatoes, chilled stock, or water. Refrigerate.

3. Serve gazpacho chilled with a topping of crisp croutons or sour cream and chopped green onions.

Serves 8.

TIPS:

• The gazpacho will keep 2–3 days in the fridge.

• It's a delicious addition to a picnic. Take it along in a Thermos, adding a couple of ice cubes to keep the soup nice and cold.

• Mugs and cups are handy for serving soups when there's a crowd and the stock of bowls runs low, or outside, when bowls and spoons are a nuisance.

Pan Bagnat

1	long, crusty French *or* **Italian loaf**	
3	firm, ripe tomatoes, *sliced*	
½	sweet onion, *thinly sliced*	
1	green pepper, *thinly sliced*	
1	red pepper, *thinly sliced*	
2	hard-boiled eggs, *sliced*	
2–3	anchovy fillets, *rinsed and chopped (optional)*	
¼ cup	black olives, *pitted and chopped (optional)*	60 ml

Dressing

1 tbsp	balsamic vinegar	15 ml
½ tsp	Dijon-style mustard	2 ml
1 clove	garlic, *minced*	
¼ cup	olive oil	60 ml
	salt and freshly ground black pepper	

A multi-layered sandwich with Mediterranean flavours, pan bagnat originated in Nice and literally means "moist bread" in the Provençal dialect. It should be assembled the day before, to give the flavours time to blend – making it perfect for a picnic or lunch in the middle of a busy day. The fillings can be varied to suit your taste – but don't get too complicated. Maybe just add a layer of sliced provolone or thinly sliced chicken.

1. Combine ingredients for dressing, seasoning to taste.

2. Slice bread in half horizontally. Scoop out a little of the soft bread to make room for the filling. Brush each half with dressing.

3. Start building the sandwich on the bottom half – layers of tomato, onion, peppers, egg, anchovy, and olives; season with salt and pepper as you go.

4. Put the top half of the bread in place and press down to squeeze the layers together.

5. Wrap tightly in foil and refrigerate overnight, or at least for a few hours. Cut in slices to serve.

Serves 2–4.

TIPS:

• If you happen to have some fresh basil, put a few leaves on the tomato slices.

• If you don't have balsamic vinegar, substitute a dash of lemon juice or red wine or sherry vinegar.

Red Clam Chowder

2 tbsp	**olive oil**	30 ml
½ cup	**smoked ham** *or* **bacon,** *chopped*	125 ml
2	**medium onions,** *finely chopped*	
2	**cloves garlic,** *chopped*	
2	**stalks celery,** *chopped*	
2	**medium potatoes,** *peeled and diced*	
½ tsp	**hot pepper flakes**	2 ml
1 tsp	**dried thyme**	5 ml
	salt and freshly ground pepper	
1 can	**plum tomatoes,** *(28 oz/796 ml), roughly chopped, with juice*	
3 cups	**chicken stock**	750 ml
2 cans	**clams,** *drained and liquid reserved (5 oz/142 g)*	
	fresh parsley, *chopped*	

TIP:

• Search the supermarket shelves for good substitutes for homemade stock: low-salt options in cans and good-quality cubes. (Knorr and Hero are 2 of the brands I like.)

As with many soups, this chowder improves in flavour if made a day or two ahead. It also freezes well, so it makes sense to cook up a good-sized batch.

1. Heat oil in a large pot. Add ham or bacon and toss over medium heat for a few minutes. Add onions and garlic and cook gently until softened. (Do not brown.)

2. Stir in celery, potatoes, hot pepper flakes, thyme, and salt and pepper, then add tomatoes and juice, stock, and the reserved liquid from the clams. Bring to a boil, lower heat, and simmer, partially covered, until vegetables are tender, about 20 minutes.

3. Add clams and simmer 5 minutes more. Adjust seasoning and serve garnished with parsley.

Serves 8.

QUICK TRICK:
Serve the Red Clam Chowder with a Cheesy Garlic Baguette: Slice a baguette in half and spread both halves with garlic butter and sprinkle with grated Parmesan cheese. Reform the loaf, smooth a little garlic butter on the outside crust, and wrap in foil. You can freeze it at this point if you wish. Heat in 400°F (200°C) oven for 10 minutes (20 minutes if frozen). Open foil and open up the bread; bake for about 5 minutes more until bread is nicely toasted.

(The Red Clam Chowder is included in the photo opposite p. 148.)

Spicy Black Bean Soup

¹/₂ lb	black turtle beans	250 g
6 cups	water	1.5 L
¹/₄ lb	pork rind *or* ham bone *(optional)*	125 g
1–2	onions, *chopped*	
2–4 cloves	garlic, *chopped (to taste)*	
1 tsp	cumin	5 ml
2 tbsp	butter	30 ml
¹/₄ lb	lean bacon *or* ham, *cubed*	125 g
2	tomatoes *(fresh or canned), peeled, seeded, and chopped*	
2–3	serrano chiles, *seeded and chopped*	
	salt and freshly ground pepper	
2 tbsp	flat-leaf parsley, *chopped*	30 ml

Rich, spicy, and rib-sticking. Serve with crisp tortilla chips, spicy croutons, or corn bread (p. 199).

1. Rinse and pick over beans, removing any debris. Cover with water in a large pot. Bring to a fast boil for 2 minutes. Remove pot from heat, cover, and leave beans for an hour.

2. Drain beans and cover with 6 cups (1.5 L) fresh water. Add pork rind or ham bone (optional), onion, garlic, and cumin. Bring contents to a boil, lower heat, partially cover, and simmer until the beans are tender, about 1¹/₂ hours.

3. Discard pork rind or ham bone. Remove about 2–3 cups (500–750 ml) beans from the pot and either blend briefly in a food processor or mash. Return the puréed beans to the pot.

4. Brown bacon or ham cubes in butter, add tomatoes and chopped chiles, and cook over moderate heat for 10 minutes. Stir mixture into beans and simmer all together for 15 minutes or so. Adjust seasoning. Serve hot, sprinkled with parsley.

Serves 6.

TIP:

•Hot serrano chiles – small and light-green in colour – are occasionally available fresh, but are more readily found in cans (usually shelved with Mexican foods in the market). Or you can substitute fresh or canned jalapeños. Remove the seeds to reduce the heat, and rinse canned chiles before adding to the soup.

This Spicy Black Bean Soup is wonderful for lunch on a cool, rainy day.

VI. BREAKFAST & BRUNCH

For tips on making breakfast for a crowd, see pages 164, 166, 168, and 172.

CROWD PLEASERS:

FOR AN ELEGANT SERVE-YOURSELF BRUNCH BUFFET FOR 12

When you're expecting a bunch for brunch, this menu is ideal because it leaves you free to enjoy time with your guests: The stratas and the sticky buns are assembled the night before, and just have to be put into the oven the next day. The coffee cake can likewise be made ahead of time and just rewarmed briefly before serving.

Platter of sliced fresh fruit

Crab Strata *(p. 174)*

Sausage & Vegetable Strata *(p. 177)*

*(or make double the recipe
of one strata)*

Toasted English muffins

Caramel-Pecan Sticky Buns *(p. 210)*

and

Blueberry Streusel Coffee Cake
(p. 207)

EASY EGGS FOR EIGHT

This is an easy twist on the traditional scrambled eggs, ham, and toast breakfast. The piperade – a recipe of Basque origins that's a combination of ham, peppers, and tomatoes – can be made a day or two ahead. Just re-heat it as you're scrambling the eggs. The cornbread mixes up in minutes – especially if you combine the dry ingredients ahead of time and store them in a plastic container.

Fresh fruit or fruit juices

Piperade with Eggs *(p. 176)*

Sliced corn bread or corn bread
muffins *(p.199)*

and

Whole-wheat toast

Basic Buttermilk Pancakes

2 cups	buttermilk	500 ml
2	large eggs, *beaten*	
1 tsp	vanilla	5 ml
6 tbsp	butter, *melted and cooled*	90 ml
1½ cups	all-purpose flour	375 ml
½ tsp	salt	2 ml
2 tsp	baking soda	10 ml
¼ cup	butter *(for cooking pancakes)*	60 ml

Pancakes are high on everyone's list of favourite breakfast foods. Although most kitchen cupboards hold a box of pancake mix, this from-scratch version has several advantages: The batter can be made ahead of time and kept (covered) in the refrigerator for a day or two. And you can make interesting variations by replacing part of the all-purpose flour with whole-wheat, buckwheat, rye, or even corn meal. Serve the pancakes with one of the syrups on the facing page.

1. Combine buttermilk, eggs, vanilla, and melted butter. Combine dry ingredients and gently stir into buttermilk mixture until just blended – don't overmix. Set batter aside, covered, in the refrigerator until needed.

2. Brush surface of a large, non-stick frying pan with butter. When the pan is hot, spoon in batter, spreading each scoop to form a 4" (10-cm) circle; don't crowd the pan. Cook for a few minutes over medium-high heat; when the tops of the pancakes begin to form a smooth skin with small bubbles on the surface, turn them over and cook briefly to brown the other side.

Makes about 12 generous-sized pancakes.

MAKING BREAKFAST FOR A BUNCH:
•When cooking a lot of pancakes, French toast, or omelettes, keep a small pot of melted butter and a pastry brush nearby so you can quickly grease the pan between batches.

A Duo of Pancake Syrups

Blueberry Syrup

½ cup	sugar	125 ml
1 cup	water	250 ml
2 cups	wild blueberries	500 ml
	juice of ½ lemon	

TIP:

•Stored in a covered jar in the refrigerator, the syrup will keep several weeks.

Spiced Maple Syrup

½ cup	maple syrup	125 ml
1 strip	lemon zest	
pinch	nutmeg	
2 tbsp	butter	30 ml
	pecans, *toasted and chopped (optional)*	

TIP:

• The spiced maple syrup can also be served over sliced peaches, nectarines, or apples browned lightly in butter. Vary the spice according to the fruit: cinnamon with apples, a hint of ginger (freshly grated would be wonderful) with peaches or nectarines.

Blueberry Syrup

Wild blueberries make a wonderful syrup for pancakes, waffles, or ice cream. Use the same technique with raspberries, or a combination of berries.

1. Dissolve sugar in water in a small pot over medium heat. Simmer syrup for 10 minutes.

2. Add blueberries and lemon juice, and simmer until berries are tender.

3. Whirl in a food processor or smash with a fork.

Makes 1½ cups (375 ml).

Spiced Maple Syrup

Given how wonderful pure maple syrup tastes without anything added to it, this is perhaps gilding the lily. But it sure is delicious.

1. Combine maple syrup, lemon zest, and nutmeg in a small saucepan. Heat for several minutes, but do not boil.

2. Remove pan from heat and swirl in butter. Add nuts if you like, or use them as a garnish.

Makes a generous ¹/₂ cup (125 ml).

 QUICK TRICK:

Maple butter makes a delicious spread for toast or scones: Cream ¹/₄ cup (60 ml) butter until fluffy, then gradually beat in 2 tbsp (30 ml) of maple syrup.

French Toast with a Kick

4	eggs	
1½ cups	milk, *preferably homogenized*	375 ml
¼ cup	Irish cream liqueur	60 ml
1 tbsp	granulated sugar	15 ml
½ tsp	vanilla	2 ml
2 tbsp	butter, *melted*	30 ml
8–10 slices raisin bread		
	butter *(for frying)*	
	cinnamon *(optional)*	

Irish cream liqueur is what makes this French toast a little different.

1. Beat eggs, milk, liqueur, sugar, vanilla, and butter in a large bowl until smooth.

2. Dip bread quickly into egg mixture, and pan fry in hot butter until golden brown on both sides. Sprinkle lightly with cinnamon, if desired. Serve hot with syrup.

Serves 4.

MAKING BREAKFAST FOR A BUNCH:

•One essential piece of equipment is a large frying pan with a non-stick surface. Electric models are ideal because they provide even, easily regulated heat. Also, since they can be plugged in anywhere, they free up space at the stove.

Raisin bread and a bit of Irish cream liqueur are the secret to this fabulous French toast.

French Toast with Fresh Peaches

Topping

4	fresh peaches	
¼ cup	maple syrup	60 ml

French toast

5	eggs	
⅔ cup	cream *or* milk	175 ml
1 tbsp	sugar	15 ml
dash	vanilla	
½ tsp	orange rind, *grated* (optional)	2 ml
8 slices	egg bread	
	butter (*for frying*)	

Instead of the usual white bread, try slices of egg bread or even stale croissants to make memorable French toast. And have real maple syrup on hand – there's a world of difference in taste between it and the artificially flavoured stuff.

1. Dip peaches briefly in boiling water to loosen skins; peel and slice. Toss with maple syrup and set aside.

2. Combine eggs, cream, sugar, vanilla, and grated orange rind, and pour into a shallow dish.

3. Dip bread slices into the egg mixture to coat both sides. Melt butter in a large non-stick frying pan over moderate heat and fry bread slices until golden on both sides. Serve hot with peaches and maple syrup.

Serves 4.

MAKING BREAKFAST FOR A BUNCH:

• When preparing French toast for a crowd, set the dipped bread in a single layer on a baking sheet, ready to go into the frying pan when the previous batch of slices is removed.

Pan-Fried Fish

1½ lbs	fish fillets	750 g
	flour	
	salt and freshly ground pepper	
2	eggs	
¼ cup	milk	60 ml
6 tbsp	unsalted butter	90 ml
	juice of 1 lemon	
	fresh parsley, *chopped*	

If the anglers get lucky early in the morning, try cooking the catch this way for breakfast. It's the easiest and perhaps the best way to enjoy freshly caught fish. Wonderful with home fries or a wedge of Hash-Brown Pancake (p. 125) and warm corn meal muffins (p. 199).

1. Season flour with a dash of salt and pepper. Beat eggs and milk together lightly. Dip fish fillets one at a time into the seasoned flour, then into the egg mixture, and then again into the flour, dusting off excess.

2. Heat 3 tbsp (45 ml) butter in a large, heavy skillet over moderate heat. Sauté fish until lightly browned on one side, about 5 minutes; turn over and cook other side. The fish is done when the flesh becomes opaque and separates into moist flakes.

3. Remove fish from pan and pour away cooking fat. Add lemon juice and remaining butter to the pan, and cook until butter melts. Pour sauce over fish, season to taste, and sprinkle with parsley. Enjoy at once.

Serves 4.

TIPS:

• If you're also preparing bacon, fry the fillets in the bacon fat instead of butter.

• The fish is equally delicious when it's dipped only in flour (no eggs or milk) and then sautéed.

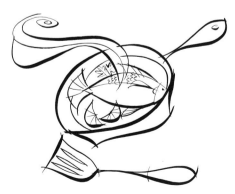

Overleaf: The classic cottage breakfast – pan-fried fish with fried onions and potatoes.

Special Scrambled Eggs

¼ cup	butter	60 ml
8	eggs	
2 tbsp	milk *or* cream	30 ml
	salt and freshly ground pepper	

Additions

smoked salmon, *slivered,*
with fresh dill *or* chives, *chopped*

---

mushrooms, *sliced and sautéed in butter,*
with green onions and a squeeze of lemon juice

QUICK TRICK:

Fried tomatoes make the perfect accompaniment to scrambled eggs, sausages, and hash browns: Cut firm tomatoes into eighths. Heat equal amounts of butter and oil until very hot in a large frying pan. Sprinkle tomato wedges with a little salt and cook until nicely browned on one side, then turn and brown the other side (about 2–3 minutes per side); remove with a slotted spoon. Add a couple of splashes of balsamic vinegar to juices in pan and stir. Pour over tomatoes and sprinkle with some chopped herbs and freshly ground pepper.

The secret to creamy scrambled eggs is diligent stirring over gentle heat. If you try to hurry them up, they turn instantly dry and lumpy.

1. Melt butter in a non-stick frying pan. Beat eggs with a dash of salt and pour into pan.

2. Stir constantly over moderate-to-low heat until eggs thicken to creamy consistency. Lift pan from heat and stir in milk or cream and smoked salmon or mushrooms as desired.

3. Season with salt and pepper and serve at once.

Serves 4.

TIP:

• For extra-creamy eggs with a bit of a tang, replace the cream with 2 tbsp (30 ml) soft cream cheese.

MAKING BREAKFAST FOR A BUNCH:

• The most convenient way to cook bacon for a crowd is to broil it instead of frying. Preheat broiler, spread bacon on the rack of the broiler pan, and put a cup of water in the pan to catch the fat and prevent flare-ups. Place the pan about 5" (13 cm) from the heat. Keep watch. When one side is lightly browned (about 3 minutes), turn the strips over and brown the other side. Remove to a tray lined with paper towel to drain off excess fat, and keep warm in the oven.

• Delegate the tasks of broiling the bacon, making coffee and toast, and setting the table to helpers. A designated toast butterer is also helpful.

Huevos Rancheros

2 cups	red *or* green salsa	500 ml
6	medium corn or wheat tortillas (8"/20 cm)	
3 tbsp	butter	45 ml
6	eggs	
handful	fresh coriander, *chopped, for garnish (optional)*	

Eggs and tomatoes were meant for each other. In this traditional Mexican dish, fried eggs are topped with salsa. You can make your own (see p. 41) or substitute a good store-bought one. This simple dish has become a staple for leisurely summer breakfasts.

1. Place salsa in a small saucepan to warm.

2. In a small frying pan, heat tortillas one at a time for about 30 seconds per side to warm and soften. Stack and wrap in a towel to keep warm.

3. Heat butter in a large frying pan over medium heat. Break eggs one at a time into a saucer and slip them into the hot butter. Tip and shake the pan a little – just like at the diner – to keep the eggs from sticking and to flip a little hot butter over them to cook the tops.

4. Place a tortilla on a warm plate. Top with a fried egg, spoon salsa on egg, and sprinkle with chopped coriander if desired.

Makes 6.

QUICK TRICK:
A cold continental-style breakfast is sometimes a nice alternative: Bagels with deli-style cream cheese, slices of smoked salmon, capers, raw onion rings, and lemon slices are a traditional favourite. Or put out slices of mild, nutty cheeses (Emmenthal, Gruyère, Fontina, Jarlsberg, and Gouda) and sliced ham, or perhaps some smoked trout. Add a basket of rye, pumpernickel, and walnut breads.

Crab Strata

1 loaf	**French bread,** *cut in* *¹/₂" (1-cm) slices on the* *diagonal*	
1 cup	**milk**	250 ml
1 pkg	**frozen leaf spinach,** *cooked, drained, and chopped*	
1 can	**crab meat,** *drained and chopped (4.2 oz/120 g)*	
2 tbsp	**butter**	30 ml
2 tbsp	**green onions,** *chopped*	30 ml
½ tsp	**dried thyme**	2 ml
1 cup	**Swiss** *or* **mild Cheddar cheese,** *grated*	250 ml
4	**eggs**	
	salt and freshly ground pepper	
½ cup	**35% cream**	125 ml

A perfect dish when something special is required. Although it's elegant and takes a little time to prepare, it's not at all complicated. Plus, the work is done the night before and the strata just popped into the oven the next morning.

1. The night before serving, dip bread slices in milk and gently press out as much liquid as possible. Arrange a layer of bread slices in the bottom of a buttered oven-proof dish approximately 8" x 8" (20 cm x 20 cm).

2. Melt butter in a skillet and cook onions until soft over moderate heat. Add the crab meat and thyme, and heat for a few minutes. Season with salt and pepper.

3. Layer half the spinach on top of the bread slices, then half the crab mixture and one-third of the cheese. Repeat layers with remaining ingredients, ending with a layer of bread and cheese.

4. Beat eggs with salt and pepper and pour over layers. Cover with plastic wrap and leave overnight in the refrigerator.

5. The following day, bring to room temperature. Pour a layer of cream over the top. Bake at 350°F (180°C) until puffed and lightly browned, about 40–50 minutes. Serve hot.

Serves 6.

QUICK TRICK:

Mimosas – half fresh orange juice, half sparkling white wine – make an easy, elegant addition to brunch.

Zucchini Frittata

2 tbsp	olive oil	30 ml
1 clove	garlic, *sliced*	
2	zucchini, *trimmed and thinly sliced*	
	salt and freshly ground pepper	
2	green onions, *finely chopped*	
½ cup	parsley, *finely chopped*	125 ml
10	eggs, *lightly beaten*	
3 tbsp	butter	45 ml
½ cup	Swiss cheese, *grated*	125 ml

TIP:

•To save a bit of time in the morning, Step 1 can be done the night before and the zucchini mixture refrigerated.

This Italian-style omelette is quickly prepared, hearty enough to feed a group, and very flexible, since you can combine odds and ends of vegetables and cheese, or even add a can of artichoke hearts or sliced pimientos from the cupboard.

1. Heat oil in a small frying pan and toss in garlic. When it has coloured, scoop it out and discard. Add zucchini and toss over medium heat until browned. Season lightly and sprinkle with green onions and half the parsley.

2. Combine eggs and zucchini mixture, and season with salt and pepper.

3. Preheat broiler. Over medium-high heat, melt 2 tbsp (30 ml) butter in a large (about 10"/26-cm) well-seasoned or non-stick pan that can go into the oven. Pour in egg mixture. Leave for a couple of minutes to set the bottom, then shake pan gently over the heat.

4. When underside is lightly browned and top is still runny (another minute or two), sprinkle cheese on top and dot with remaining butter. Slide frittata under the broiler until cheese melts and the top starts to brown. Cut in wedges, sprinkle with the rest of the parsley, and serve at once.

Serves 4–5.

Piperade with Eggs

½–¾ cup	butter	125–175 ml
16–20	eggs	
	fresh parsley, *chopped*	

Piperade

2 tbsp	olive oil	30 ml
½ lb	cooked smoked ham, *thinly sliced and cut in strips*	250 g
1	onion, *finely chopped*	
2 cloves	garlic, *minced*	
2	green peppers, *seeded and sliced*	
2	red peppers, *seeded and sliced*	
2 lbs	firm ripe tomatoes, *seeded and chopped* or	1 kg
1 can	plum tomatoes, *drained and chopped (28 oz/796 ml)*	
1 tbsp	fresh basil, *chopped* or	15 ml
1 tsp	each dried basil and oregano	5 ml
2 dashes	hot sauce	
	salt and freshly ground pepper	

Piperade is a savoury mixture of peppers and tomatoes that captures the flavours of summer and is particularly good with eggs. Tuck spoonfuls of it into omelettes, or pile it in the centre of a platter of scrambled eggs for an easy breakfast dish for a crowd. Serve with hot corn bread (p. 199), brioche, or whole-grain toast.

1. Make the piperade: Heat oil in a large frying pan. Add ham strips, brown lightly, then lift out and reserve.

2. Add onion and garlic to the pan and cook until soft. Toss in pepper strips and cook until lightly browned and beginning to soften.

3. Add tomatoes, herbs, and seasonings, and stir over moderately high heat for a few minutes until most of the liquid has evaporated. Return ham to pan, partially cover, and set aside until needed.

4. Whisk the eggs with a little salt in two batches of 8–10. Melt half the butter in a non-stick frying pan, pour in one batch of eggs, and stir constantly over medium heat until eggs are set and creamy. Turn out onto a large platter and keep warm. Cook the second batch of eggs in the remaining butter and add to the platter.

5. Reheat the piperade and pile in the middle. Sprinkle with pepper and parsley, and serve at once.

Serves 8.

TIP:
•The piperade (Steps 1–3) can be made up to 2 days ahead and kept refrigerated.

Sausage & Vegetable Strata

1 loaf	**French bread,** *cut in ¹⁄₂" (1-cm) slices on the diagonal*	
1 cup	**milk**	250 ml
1 tbsp	**olive oil**	15 ml
2–3	**Italian sausages**	
	Piperade *(recipe on facing page, made without ham)*	
1 cup	**Cheddar cheese,** *grated*	250 ml
4	**eggs,** *beaten*	
	salt and freshly ground pepper	
1 tbsp	**butter**	15 ml

TIPS:

• Make up a double batch of piperade and serve some alongside the strata. Add a platter of grilled sausages, and you've got an easy Sunday supper.

• If you have any mushrooms in the fridge, you can sauté them and add them to the strata as well.

When surprise guests show up and you have to make something out of nothing, a hunt in the refrigerator may reveal a couple of sausages, a few eggs, and a vegetable or two that can be turned into a special breakfast dish. Assemble it the night before and pop it in the oven in the morning.

1. The night before serving, dip bread slices in milk and gently press out excess liquid. Arrange a layer of slices in the bottom of a buttered oven-proof dish, approximately 8" x 8" (20 cm x 20 cm).

2. Remove sausage meat from casings. Heat oil in a large frying pan. Add sausage meat, breaking it up with a fork, and cook until lightly browned. Remove meat with a slotted spoon and pour away excess fat.

3. Prepare the piperade in the same pan, omitting the ham.

4. Layer half the sausage on top of the bread slices, then add half the piperade and a third of the cheese. Repeat the layers with remaining ingredients, ending with a layer of bread and cheese.

5. Beat eggs with salt and pepper and pour over the layers. Cover with plastic wrap and refrigerate.

6. The next day, bring the strata to room temperature and dot the top with butter. Bake at 350°F (180°C) until puffed and lightly browned, about 40–45 minutes. Serve hot.

Serves 6.

VII. BAKED THINGS & DESSERTS

KID PLEASERS:

NO COMPLAINTS WHEN YOU ASK FOR A HAND MAKING THESE

It's amazing how much help from the kids suddenly materializes when it comes to dessert. These quick and easy recipes are particularly suited to young cooks – although somehow the yield may diminish before serving time:

Apple-Blackberry Crisp

5 cups	tart apples	1.25 L
	(approximately), peeled and sliced	
1 cup	blackberries	250 ml
1 tbsp	lemon juice	15 ml
	sugar to taste	
	(about 1/3 cup/75 ml)	

Topping

1/4 cup	flour	60 ml
1/2 cup	large-flake oats	125 ml
2/3 cup	brown sugar	150 ml
pinch	each salt and ground cloves	
1 tsp	cinnamon	5 ml
1/3 cup	cold butter	75 ml
1/2 cup	almonds, *slivered*	125 ml

Delicious warm from the oven – with a little vanilla ice cream or lightly whipped cream, naturally! If blackberries are not available, you may find mulberries or loganberries; even chopped cranberries – or apples alone – will taste wonderful.

1. Toss apples, blackberries, lemon juice, and sugar together and place in a well-buttered 9" x 13" (23-cm x 33-cm) baking dish.

2. In a large bowl combine flour, oats, brown sugar, and spices. Cut in cold butter until mixture resembles coarse crumbs. (Or combine in a food processor using on/off pulses.) Stir in nuts. Spread evenly over fruit.

3. Bake at 350°F (180°C) for about 45 minutes, until fruit is tender and topping is crisp and nicely browned.

Serves 8.

TIPS:

• Peaches and blueberries make another great combination. Leave out the cloves in the topping and substitute chopped toasted pecans for the almonds.

• If you don't have any whipping cream on hand, lightly sweeten some sour cream or plain yoghurt to serve with the crisp.

Chocolate Chunk Shortbreads

1 cup	unsalted butter	250 ml
½ cup	fine sugar	125 ml
1 tsp	vanilla	5 ml
1¾ cups	all-purpose flour	450 ml
¼ cup	rice flour *or* cornstarch	60 ml
1 cup	semi-sweet chocolate chunks *(plus additional for decorating; optional)*	250 ml

A sophisticated variation of the chocolate chip cookie. These shortbreads keep well and have a pleasing crunch.

1. Cream butter, sugar, and vanilla until light.

2. Combine flours (or flour and cornstarch), and blend into creamed mixture. Do not overmix. Add chocolate chunks.

3. Pinch off a tablespoon or so of mixture and place on lightly buttered and floured cookie sheet. Press roughly into shape with two fingers and top with an extra chocolate chunk if you like.

4. Bake at 325°F (160°C) until firm but not brown, about 15–20 minutes.

Makes 16 cookies.

Peach & Blueberry Shortcakes

Filling

6	large, ripe peaches	
	peeled	
1 cup	blueberries	250 ml
	sugar *or*	
	maple syrup, *to taste*	

Shortcakes

2 cups	all-purpose flour	500 ml
1 tbsp	baking powder	15 ml
1 tsp	salt	5 ml
2 tbsp	sugar	30 ml
¼ cup	butter	60 ml
⅔ cup	milk	150 ml
1 cup	35% cream,	250 ml
	whipped	

TIP:

• Substitute raspberries for the blueberries, or use a combination of raspberries and blueberries.

Shortcakes are not just for strawberries. This recipe combines peaches and blueberries – which look and taste wonderful together – in individual little cakes.

1. Cut peaches in half, remove pits, and slice. Toss them with blueberries and a little sugar or maple syrup, and let stand for a while at room temperature.

2. In a mixing bowl stir together flour, baking powder, salt, and sugar. Cut in butter until mixture resembles coarse crumbs. Add milk gradually, tossing mixture gently with a fork to form a soft dough.

3. Turn dough out onto a lightly floured surface and pat into an even layer about ½" (1 cm) thick. Cut into 8 rounds. Brush tops with a little cream and sprinkle with sugar.

4. Bake in a 425°F (220°C) oven for 15 minutes, or until nicely browned and cooked through.

5. Split the shortcakes while they're still warm. Pile sweetened fruit on the bottom half of each shortcake, replace the other half, and top with lightly whipped cream and more fruit. Enjoy immediately.

Serves 8.

TIPS:

• The shortcakes can be made the day before serving. Cool, then wrap well in foil. Warm briefly before serving.

• The best way to remove the skins from peaches is to drop them, one at a time, into boiling water for 30 seconds. Remove and immediately plunge into ice water for a few seconds. The skins should slip off easily.

These individual Peach & Blueberry Shortcakes capture the look and taste of summer, and are just about impossible to resist.

Refrigerator-Rise Potato Bread

2	medium potatoes	
6–7 cups	all-purpose flour	1.5–1.75 L
2 tbsp	Fleischmann's Quick-Rise Instant Yeast *or* RapidRise Instant Yeast *(2 envelopes)* *(see Tip, facing page)*	30 ml
½ cup	sugar	125 ml
¼ cup	skim-milk powder	60 ml
1½ tsp	salt	7 ml
½ cup	butter	125 ml
2	eggs *(at room temperature)*	
	milk *or* egg white *(for brushing tops of bread and buns)*	

This is an extremely handy recipe if you have a summer place located far from a source of good, fresh baking. Make the multi-purpose dough at leisure on a cool evening, then use as needed for bread, hamburger buns, or fabulous pecan sticky buns (p. 188). Although the dough has to rise for at least 3 hours, it does so in the refrigerator, and it can stay for up to 36 hours before being used.

1. Cook potatoes in at least 3 cups (750 ml) water. Drain, saving the potato-cooking water, and mash until smooth. You should have about 1 cup (250 ml) of mashed potatoes. Set aside.

2. Combine 2 cups (500 ml) flour, yeast, sugar, milk powder, and salt in a large bowl. Heat 1½ cups (375 ml) of the reserved potato-cooking water, butter, and the mashed potatoes to 125°F (50°C). With electric mixer at low speed or a large spoon, mix the hot liquid into dry ingredients until blended, then beat vigorously for 2 minutes. Add eggs and beat 2 minutes more.

3. Using a large spoon, add 3–3½ cups (750–875 ml) more flour and combine to make a soft, moist dough. Turn out on a lightly floured surface, and knead for 4 or 5 minutes until dough is smooth and elastic, adding more flour as necessary to keep the dough workable. (You may not use all of it.)

4. Shape dough into a ball and put in a large, lightly greased bowl. (Turn the dough so the surface is greased.) Cover bowl with a slightly damp tea towel, or plastic wrap, and set aside in a warm spot for 20 minutes.

5. Punch dough down and knead briefly in bowl. Shape into a ball, turn to grease top, cover bowl tightly with plastic wrap, and put in the refrigerator for at least 3 hours or up to 36 hours.

TIP:

• The dough rises up to 50% faster when you use Quick-Rise Instant Yeast (the name given to the Fleischmann's brand of fast-acting yeast in Canada, and the one most available in Canadian supermarkets; in the U.S., substitute the same amount of Fleischmann's RapidRise Instant Yeast). These instant yeasts do not have to be dissolved in water, but rather can be mixed in directly with the other dry ingredients.

Bread

1. When ready to bake, remove dough from refrigerator, punch down, and knead briefly in the bowl.

2. Divide dough in half and, with well-greased hands, form into two loaves. (See p. 189 for technique.) Place in well-greased loaf pans, cover with a damp tea towel, and set in a warm spot for about 30 minutes.

3. For a soft surface, brush tops with milk; for a crisper, glazed top, brush with beaten egg white. Bake in preheated 375°F (190°C) oven for about 30 minutes. Turn out on racks to cool. Tops should be nicely browned and bottoms should sound hollow when tapped.

Makes 2 loaves.

Hamburger Buns

1. When ready to bake, remove dough from refrigerator, punch down, knead briefly in the bowl, and divide in half. Cut each half into 8 or 9 equal pieces.

2. With greased hands, form each piece into a smooth ball, set on a well-greased baking sheet, and press to flatten slightly. Cover with a slightly damp tea towel and leave in a warm spot for about 25 minutes.

3. For a soft surface, brush buns with milk; for a crisper, glazed top, brush with beaten egg white. Bake in preheated 375°F (190°C) oven for about 15 minutes until tops are nicely browned and rolls sound hollow when tapped.

Makes about 1¹/₂ dozen buns.

Overleaf, clockwise from upper left: Whole-Wheat Honey Bread (p. 189), Raisin Soda Bread (p. 203), Refrigerator-Rise Potato Bread (this page), more Whole-Wheat Honey Bread, Refrigerator-Rise Sticky Buns (p. 188), and Speedy Pizza (p. 190).

Refrigerator-Rise Sticky Buns

| 1 recipe | Refrigerator-Rise Potato Bread dough *(recipe on p. 184)* | |

Filling

1/2 cup	sugar	125 ml
2 tsp	cinnamon	10 ml
1/4 cup	butter, *melted*	60 ml
1 cup	raisins *(optional)*	250 ml

Topping

6 tbsp	butter	90 ml
1 cup	corn syrup	250 ml
1½ cups	dark brown sugar *(packed)*	375 ml
2¼ cups	pecans, *chopped*	560 ml

Served warm from the oven, these sticky buns will quickly become a favourite morning treat.

1. Prepare dough through Step 5. When ready to bake buns, punch dough down and divide in half.

2. On a lightly floured surface, roll out each half into a rectangle approximately 10" x 16" (25 cm x 40 cm) and about 1/4" (6 mm) thick. Combine cinnamon and sugar. Brush dough with melted butter, and sprinkle with the cinnamon-sugar mixture and raisins if you like.

3. Starting from the shorter side, roll up dough jelly-roll fashion. Pinch seam to seal. Cut each roll into generous 1/2" (1-cm) slices. (You should have a total of 27 slices.)

4. Butter 3 round 8" (20-cm) pans, using 2 tbsp (30 ml) of butter on each. Spread the bottom of each with 1/3 of the corn syrup, 1/3 of the brown sugar, and 1/3 of the pecans. Lay 9 of the slices in each of the prepared pans. Let stand, covered with a damp tea towel, in a warm, draft-free spot for about 25 minutes.

5. Bake 25–30 minutes in preheated 375°F (190°C) oven until golden on top and springy to the touch. Immediately turn out onto serving platters. Serve warm.

Makes 27 buns.

TIP:
• Sticky buns can be frozen and reheated.

(The Refrigerator-Rise Sticky Buns are shown in the photo on the previous page.)

Whole-Wheat Honey Bread

3½ cups	all-purpose flour *(approximately)*	875 ml
2 tbsp	Fleischmann's Quick-Rise Instant Yeast *or* RapidRise Instant Yeast *(2 envelopes)* *(see Tip, p. 185)*	30 ml
⅔ cup	skim-milk powder	150 ml
2 tsp	salt	10 ml
2 cups	water	500 ml
⅓ cup	honey	75 ml
¼ cup	butter	60 ml
1	egg *(at room temperature)*	
2 cups	whole-wheat flour	500 ml
	milk *for brushing tops of loaves*	

TIP:

• After mastering the basic method, replace up to 1 cup (250 ml) of the whole-wheat flour with another grain – such as rye or oats – or muesli.

This delicious (and nutritious) bread is destined to become a cottage staple.

1. Combine 2 cups (500 ml) flour, yeast, milk powder, and salt in large bowl.

2. Heat water, honey, and butter until hot (125°F/50°C). With an electric mixer or large spoon, combine liquid and dry ingredients, then beat vigorously for 3–4 minutes. Add egg and beat for another minute.

3. Stir in whole-wheat flour with a spoon until a sticky dough forms. Knead dough on a lightly floured surface for about 5 minutes until smooth and elastic, adding remaining flour when dough gets sticky. (You may not need all the flour.) Shape dough into a ball, cover with a damp tea towel, and leave to rest for 10 minutes.

4. Grease 2 loaf pans thoroughly. Divide dough in half and, with well-greased hands, form into 2 loaves. A traditional method is to pat or roll the dough into a rectangle whose short side is slightly shorter than the pan; then, starting from the short side, roll up the dough jelly-roll fashion. Pinch the seam and ends. Place in the pans seam down and cover with a damp tea towel. Set in a very warm place until loaves double in size, about 20 minutes.

5. Brush the surface of each loaf with milk. Bake in preheated 375°F (190°C) oven for 30–35 minutes. When the loaves are done, the tops should be nicely browned and the bottoms sound hollow when tapped. Turn out on racks to cool.

Makes 2 loaves.

(The Whole-Wheat Honey Bread is shown in the photo preceeding p. 188.)

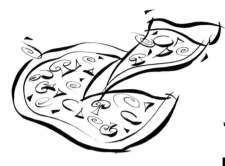

Speedy Pizza Crust

2½–3 cups all-purpose flour		625–750 ml
1 tbsp	Fleischmann's Quick-Rise Instant Yeast *or* RapidRise Instant Yeast *(1 envelope) (see Tip, p. 185)*	15 ml
¾ tsp	salt	3 ml
1 cup	water	250 ml
2 tbsp	olive oil	30 ml
	corn meal *(for dusting pans)*	

TIPS:

• Vary the flavour of the crust by replacing ½ cup (125 ml) of the all-purpose flour with whole-wheat or buckwheat flour, or corn meal.

• At the end of Step 4, the dough can be wrapped well and frozen or refrigerated for later use. Bring it to room temperature before proceeding.

When there's no pizza delivery for miles, this quick-and-easy pizza dough can be a lifesaver. If you like your pizza crust soft and thick, use this recipe to make a single 14" (35-cm) pizza. If you like a thin, crisp crust, stretch the dough out and make two 12" (30-cm) thin-crust pizzas.

1. Toss 2 cups (500 ml) flour with salt and yeast in a large bowl.

2. Heat water and oil until hot (125°F/50°C). Briskly stir or beat the liquid into the flour mixture for about 2 minutes.

3. Stir in enough remaining flour to make a soft dough. Knead on lightly floured surface until smooth and elastic, about 4 minutes, adding more flour when the dough becomes sticky. (You may not need to use all the flour.)

4. Shape dough into a smooth ball, cover, and let rest 10 minutes. Divide dough in two if you want to make thin-crust pizzas.

5. Grease pizza pans or baking sheets well and dust with corn meal. Stretch or roll dough to fit. Cover with your favourite toppings and bake in preheated 400°F (200°C) oven for 20–30 minutes until crust is nicely browned and topping is piping hot.

Makes one 14" (35-cm) thick-crust pizza or two 12" (30-cm) thin-crust pizzas.

(The Speedy Pizza is shown in the photo preceeding p. 188.)

One-Pot Brownies
with Chocolate Marshmallow Topping

Brownies

2 oz	**unsweetened chocolate** (*2 squares*)	**56 g**
1/3 cup	**butter**	**75 ml**
1 cup	**sugar**	**250 ml**
2	**eggs**	
1/2 tsp	**vanilla**	**2 ml**
3/4 cup	**flour**	**175 ml**
1/2 tsp	**baking powder**	**2 ml**
1/2 tsp	**salt**	**2 ml**
1/2 cup	**nuts,** *chopped*	**125 ml**

Topping

5	**large marshmallows,** *sliced in half*	
2 tbsp	**butter**	**30 ml**
1 oz	**unsweetened chocolate** (*1 square*)	**28 g**
1/4 cup	**water or milk**	**60 ml**
1 1/4 cups	**icing sugar**	**300 ml**
1/2 tsp	**vanilla**	**2 ml**

This comes from the collection of one of the best cottage cooks I know. She has a special talent for effortlessly bringing out one yummy treat after another. Her version of the all-time favourite fudgy square can be stirred up in just one pot.

1. In a medium saucepan melt chocolate and butter. Add sugar, eggs, and vanilla, and stir until smooth.

2. Stir in flour, baking powder, salt, and nuts.

3. Spread mixture in a lightly greased 9" x 9" (23-cm x 23-cm) pan. Bake in 350°F (180°C) oven for about 20 minutes, or until the brownies dimple slightly when you press the centre of the pan.

4. Remove from the oven and place the marshmallows on top, cut side down.

5. In the brownie-making saucepan (wash first), melt chocolate for topping with butter over low heat. Add water or milk, then stir in icing sugar until mixture is smooth. Stir in vanilla.

6. Drizzle icing over and around the marshmallows. Leave to cool before cutting into squares.

Makes 36.

TIP:
• If you're going to have a campfire, leave the Chocolate Marshmallow Topping off the brownies. Then hand out roasting sticks and marshmallows around the fire and let people top their brownies with warm, gooey toasted marshmallows.

Sandy's Orange Muffins

1 cup	crushed bran flakes	250 ml
1 cup	quick oats	250 ml
1 cup	100% bran cereal	250 ml
1 cup	boiling water	250 ml
2	oranges, *grated rind*	
1 cup	orange juice	250 ml
½ cup	shortening	125 ml
1½ cups	sugar	375 ml
2	eggs	
2 cups	buttermilk	500 ml
1 tsp	vanilla	5 ml
2½ cups	all-purpose flour	625 ml
4 tsp	baking soda	20 ml
pinch	salt	
1 cup	raisins	250 ml
1 cup	dates, *chopped*	250 ml

Topping (optional)

2 tbsp	sugar	30 ml
¼ tsp	cinnamon	1 ml

Keep a batch of batter in the fridge for these moist orange-bran muffins, and enjoy them fresh-baked at a moment's notice: All you have to do is grease the muffin tins and spoon in the batter. The batter will keep for up to 4 weeks.

1. Combine first six ingredients in a large bowl, mix well, and set aside to cool.

2. Cream shortening and sugar in a large bowl; add eggs, buttermilk, and vanilla, and beat until smooth.

3. Combine flour, baking soda, and salt. Stir into creamed mixture and mix lightly to blend. Stir this mixture into orange mixture along with raisins and dates. Mix well. Store in a covered container in the refrigerator for at least one day before baking.

4. To bake, fill greased muffin cups ¾ full. Sprinkle with topping mixture, if desired. Bake at 400°F (200°C) for 18–25 minutes, or until top springs back when lightly touched.

Makes about 2½-dozen muffins.

TIPS:

• Vary the 2 cups (500 ml) of fruit to suit your taste – and to use what you have on hand: Try raisins only, dates only, or a mixture with dried apricots. Or put in fresh fruit, such as blueberries.

• For long storage, make up plain batter, then mix in the fruit of your choice when ready to bake.

• If you want to use up the buttermilk, or have a real crowd to feed, this recipe can be doubled without a problem.

Double-Chocolate Peanut Bars

½ cup	peanut butter	125 ml
⅓ cup	corn syrup	75 ml
⅓ cup	honey	75 ml
½ cup	cocoa	125 ml
¼ cup	brown sugar, *lightly packed*	60 ml
3 cups	miniature marshmallows	750 ml
1 tsp	vanilla	5 ml
3 cups	crisp rice cereal	750 ml
1 cup	peanuts	250 ml
1–1½ cups	semi-sweet chocolate chips	250–375 ml

This is the perfect cottage goodie: You don't have to turn on the oven, and it takes only minutes to make. What's more, the combination of chocolate and peanut butter is irresistible to kids of all ages.

1. Combine the first 5 ingredients in a large saucepan. Heat, stirring constantly, until smooth and almost boiling. Reduce heat to low, add marshmallows, and stir constantly until mixture is melted and smooth.

2. Remove from heat. Stir in vanilla, cereal, and peanuts, and mix well. Press firmly into a greased 8" (20-cm) or 9" (23-cm) square pan.

3. Melt chocolate chips and spread evenly over bars. Cool until chocolate is set. Cut into squares.

Makes about 20 squares.

TIPS:

• Replace peanuts with another cup (250 ml) of cereal.

• Chocolate chips can also be sprinkled over squares and melted in the oven at 350°F (180°C) for 2–3 minutes until soft, then spread evenly over top.

At right: Double-Chocolate Peanut Bars and Sandy's Orange Muffins.

Summer Fruit Tart

2 lbs	plums	1 kg
1 cup	all-purpose flour	250 ml
1 cup	sugar	250 ml
1 tsp	baking powder	5 ml
pinch	salt	
¼ cup	butter	60 ml
1	egg, *beaten*	
1 tsp	vanilla	5 ml

Topping

3 tbsp	sugar	45 ml
3 tbsp	butter, *melted*	45 ml
1 tsp	cinnamon	5 ml
1	egg, *beaten*	

My favourite version of this tart is made with plums such as greengages, but you can substitute any fresh fruit you have on hand. It's also good, for instance, with sliced apples or peaches.

1. Halve plums, remove stones, and cut each half into equal wedges.

2. Combine flour, sugar, baking powder, and salt in a mixing bowl. Cut butter into flour until mixture resembles small crumbs; add egg and vanilla and toss together.

3. Press mixture evenly into the bottom and sides of a 9" (23-cm) pie plate. Arrange fruit in circles to cover top.

4. Bake in a 350°F (180°C) oven for 40 minutes.

5. Combine topping ingredients and spoon over hot tart. Continue baking 10–15 minutes longer until topping is set and lightly browned.

6. Serve warm or cool with lightly sweetened whipped cream, crème fraîche, or a plum sauce.

Serves 8.

QUICK TRICK:
To make a fresh plum sauce, simmer about 2 cups (500 ml) sliced plums with a little water and sugar until tender. Force the mixture through a sieve, or whirl in a food processor and then sieve to make a purée. Great with this fruit tart or over ice cream or sorbet.

Chocolate Chip Crisps

1 cup	butter	250 ml
1 cup	sugar	250 ml
¾ cup	brown sugar, *packed*	175 ml
2	eggs	
1 tsp	vanilla	5 ml
2 cups	all-purpose flour	500 ml
1½ cups	rolled oats	375 ml
1 tsp	baking soda	5 ml
¼ tsp	salt	1 ml
2 cups	crisp rice cereal	500 ml
1½ cups	chocolate chips	375 ml

TIP:

•Try butterscotch chips, raisins, or nuts instead of the chocolate chips.

Crunchy cereal makes these oatmeal chocolate chip cookies a little out of the ordinary. And this recipe makes a nice, big batch.

1. Beat butter, sugars, eggs, and vanilla in large bowl on medium speed of electric mixer until light and creamy.

2. Combine flour, oats, soda, and salt. Add to creamed mixture, mixing until blended.

3. Gently mix in cereal and chips. Drop by spoonfuls onto greased baking sheets. Bake at 375°F (190°C) for 8–12 minutes, or until lightly browned. Underbake for chewy cookies; bake longer for crisp ones. Cool on wire rack.

Makes about 5-dozen cookies.

 QUICK TRICK:

When you have the barbecue or a campfire going, Banana Boats are great fun for the kids (and the kids at heart): Peel down one or two flaps of peel and hollow out a little trench along the length of the banana. Stuff with mini-marshmallows and chocolate chips. Replace the flaps of peel, fastening them in place with toothpicks. Place the "boat" on the grill for a couple of minutes until chocolate and marshmallows melt. Eat with a spoon.

Barbecued Peaches

3 tbsp	**butter**	45 ml
5–6	**peaches,** *peeled and sliced*	
½ cup	**brown sugar,** *lightly packed*	125 ml
2 tbsp	**brandy, orange liqueur,** *or* **maple syrup**	30 ml
2 tsp	**lemon juice**	10 ml
	ice cream, sherbet, *or* **sponge cake**	

QUICK TRICK:

Use the Barbecued Peaches to make Peach Melba: Place a scoop of vanilla ice cream in an individual dessert dish. Top with some of the peach slices, drizzle with Raspberry Sauce (see Tip, p. 208), add a generous swirl of whipped cream, and top with toasted slivered almonds. Escoffier (who created this dessert for legendary soprano Nellie Melba) would be proud.

This quick, simple, and yummy dessert cooks on the barbecue while dinner is being served. Apples and nectarines – or a combination – prepared this way are also delicious.

1. Spread 1 tbsp (15 ml) of the butter in an aluminum pie plate or on a large piece of foil.

2. Toss fruit with sugar, flavouring, and lemon juice, and spoon onto buttered pie plate or foil. Dot with remaining 2 tbsp (30 ml) butter. Cover pie plate with foil and seal tightly, or fold foil around fruit, seal, and wrap with a second layer of foil.

3. Cook on barbecue, on low heat, for 20–30 minutes, or just until fruit is tender. Time will vary with the size and ripeness of the fruit. Carefully open foil, being wary of steam. Spoon fruit with juices over ice cream, sherbet, or cake.

Makes about 4 servings.

TIPS:

• A dollop of whipped cream is a nice addition when you're serving the peaches on top of cake.

• Also makes a great topping for pancakes and waffles.

• Don't worry if you leave the fruit on the barbecue for a longer time as you linger over dinner. The result will be more of a fruit sauce – but equally delicious.

• On rainy days, bake fruit in the oven at 325°F (160°C) for about 25 minutes.

The Barbecued Peaches go particularly well with vanilla ice cream.

Apricot Upside-Down Cake

¼ cup	butter	60 ml
¼ cup	brown sugar	60 ml
¼ cup	maple syrup	60 ml
1 can	apricot halves, *well drained* *(14 oz/398 ml)*	
1½ cups	all-purpose flour	375 ml
1 tsp	baking powder	5 ml
¼ tsp	baking soda	1 ml
pinch	salt	
6 tbsp	butter	90 ml
¾ cup	white sugar	175 ml
	zest of 1 lemon, *grated*	
2	eggs	
¾ cup	sour cream	175 ml

TIP:

•Substitute thinly sliced apples, pears, peaches, or nectarines for the apricots.

One of the big plusses of this delicious fruit-topped cake is that you can make it even when you don't have any fresh fruit around. Just make sure you keep a can of apricots in the cupboard.

1. Thoroughly butter a 9" (23-cm) round cake pan.

2. In a small saucepan combine ¼ cup (60 ml) butter with brown sugar and maple syrup. Stir over moderate heat until sugar is dissolved. Pour into the bottom of the cake pan and arrange apricot halves on top, cut side up.

3. Sift together flour, baking powder, baking soda, and salt. Set aside. In a mixing bowl, cream the remaining 6 tbsp (90 ml) butter with white sugar and grated lemon zest until light. Beat in eggs one at a time. Fold in flour mixture alternately with sour cream.

4. Spoon batter evenly over apricots. Bake at 350°F (180°C) for about 40 minutes, until the top is golden and a toothpick inserted in the centre comes out clean.

5. Set cake pan on a rack for 5 minutes, then loosen the edges of the cake and turn out onto a serving plate. Serve warm with whipped cream or Maple Cream (see below).

QUICK TRICK:

The Apricot Upside-Down Cake is wonderful served with Maple Cream: Beat ¾ cup (175 ml) whipping cream until soft peaks form. Gradually add ¼ cup (60 ml) maple syrup and a drop of pure vanilla. Continue beating until firm. Also try the Maple Cream on apple pie, peach pie, or a fruit crisp.

World's Best Corn Bread

1½ cups	corn meal	375 ml
1 cup	flour	250 ml
⅓ cup	sugar	75 ml
1 tbsp	baking powder	15 ml
1 tsp	salt	5 ml
1½ cups	buttermilk	375 ml
2	**eggs,** *lightly beaten*	
¾ cup	**butter,** *melted and cooled*	175 ml

The perfect quick bread to serve with eggs, chili, or southern-style barbecues. The butter in the batter is what makes this version so good.

1. Combine dry ingredients in a large bowl.

2. Lightly beat together buttermilk, eggs, and melted butter. Stir quickly into corn meal mixture; don't overmix.

3. Pour batter into a greased 9" square (23-cm) baking pan. Bake at 400°F (200°C) until golden and a toothpick inserted in the centre comes out clean, about 20–25 minutes. Serve hot.

Serves 8.

TIPS:

• Add half a roasted red pepper, chopped, and/or 2 tbsp (30 ml) of jalapeño pepper to the batter.

• Other good additions: ½ cup (125 ml) grated Cheddar or Monterey Jack cheese and ½ cup (125 ml) cooked corn kernels.

TIPS:

• To make this quick bread even quicker, combine the dry ingredients ahead of time and store in a plastic bag.

• The corn bread can be wrapped well and frozen.

• The batter also makes good muffins: Pour into greased muffin tins and bake at 400°F (200°C) for 15–20 minutes. Makes 12 large muffins.

Rosemary-Flavoured Focaccia

Speedy Pizza Crust
(recipe on p. 190)

2 tsp	dried rosemary,	10 ml
	plus a little extra for	
	sprinkling on top	
¼ cup	olive oil	60 ml
1 clove	garlic	
	coarse salt	
	corn meal (*for*	
	dusting baking sheet)	

TIPS:

• The wonderful crisp crusts typical of good country breads are just about impossible to produce in home ovens. They result from baking in brick and stone ovens with a high degree of natural humidity. Commercial ovens create this effect with a burst of steam; to get it at home, use a fine spritz of water from a spray bottle on the interior of your hot oven.

• Replace the rosemary in the dry ingredients with another herb such as thyme or basil, then put complementary toppings on the surface of the dough before the covered rising period – try goat cheese, ricotta, slivers of fresh garlic or onion, or chopped sun-dried tomatoes. Proceed with Steps 4 and 5 after rising.

Focaccia is a crusty Italian flat bread, about an inch or two high. It makes a great snack on its own, or it can be served with salads, soups, and eggs. You can prepare dozens of variations, using different combinations of herbs and toppings.

1. Slice garlic into olive oil and set aside.

2. Prepare Speedy Pizza Crust through Step 4 as described on p. 190, adding the dried rosemary to the dry ingredients.

3. Press dough into an 8" (20-cm) square or oval, about ¾" (2 cm) thick. Place on a well-greased baking sheet sprinkled with corn meal. Cover with a damp tea towel, and leave in a warm, draft-free spot until doubled in size, about 30–40 minutes.

4. Using your fingertips, press "dimples" in the surface to about three-quarters of the depth. Brush surface with some of the garlic-flavoured olive oil. Sprinkle surface of dough with a little extra rosemary and coarse salt, and mist lightly with water using a spray bottle.

5. Mist interior of a preheated 400°F (200°C) oven with a quick spritz from a spray bottle. Slip bread into the hot oven. After 5 minutes, mist oven again, then continue baking for 20–30 minutes until bread has a golden crust. Remove bread from oven and brush top with more of the olive oil. The focaccia is best eaten on the day of baking; after that, split it and toast it on the grill, brushing it first with olive oil if you like.

Makes 1 loaf.

Baking Powder Biscuits

3 cups	flour	750 ml
½ tsp	salt	2 ml
½ tsp	baking soda	2 ml
4 tsp	baking powder	20 ml
pinch	cayenne	
⅔ cup	vegetable shortening, *or* **part butter, part shortening**	175 ml
1 cup	ham, *finely diced*	250 ml
¼ cup	parsley, *finely chopped, or use a combination of fresh herbs (chives, green onions, thyme, oregano)* **or**	60 ml
1 tsp	dried thyme *or* oregano	5 ml
1 cup	buttermilk	250 ml

Egg wash

1	egg *mixed with*	
1 tbsp	milk *or* cream	15 ml

Light and tender, these are a treat to serve with eggs. The dry mix can be made quickly ahead of time in the food processor and kept in a plastic bag in the refrigerator until needed. Buttermilk makes for very light biscuits; you can use sweet milk, but omit the baking soda, or use sour milk. (For how to sour milk, see Tip, p. 203.)

1. Mix dry ingredients in a large bowl and cut in shortening to make coarse crumbs. (Or combine ingredients with short on/off pulses in a food processor.) Store the dry mix in a plastic bag in the refrigerator until needed.

2. Place mix in a large bowl with herbs and ham, sprinkle with the buttermilk, and toss all together with a fork; you may need to add an extra spoonful or two of buttermilk.

3. Drop spoonfuls of dough onto greased and floured baking sheets. Brush with egg wash and bake in a preheated 425°F (220°C) oven for 12–15 minutes.

Makes 18–20 biscuits.

TIPS:

• Omit ham and herbs; add either 1 cup (250 ml) grated Cheddar cheese, or ¼ cup (60 ml) grated Parmesan cheese with 1 tsp (5 ml) each dried thyme and oregano.

• You can also cut these biscuits into rounds: Knead the dough briefly, pat into a sheet about ½" (1 cm) thick, and cut with a 2" (5-cm) cutter. Bake as above.

(The Baking Powder Biscuits are shown as drop biscuits with grated cheese in the photo following p. 203.)

Easy Apple Cake

Topping

⅓ cup	sugar	75 ml
1½ tsp	cinnamon	7 ml

Cake

2 cups	sugar	500 ml
1 cup	vegetable oil	250 ml
4	eggs	
½ cup	orange *or* **apple juice**	125 ml
1 tbsp	vanilla	15 ml
3 cups	all-purpose flour	750 ml
1 tbsp	baking powder	15 ml
½ tsp	salt	2 ml
5	**medium apples,** *peeled, cored, and chopped*	

TIP:

• Use tart apples such as Granny Smiths for the best flavour.

Moist and delicious, with a hint of spice. This is an ideal cottage cake – it makes a large pan, needs no icing, and keeps well. It's versatile, too: Serve it for dessert, with tea, or as a coffee cake for breakfast.

1. Combine sugar and cinnamon for topping; set aside.

2. Beat first 5 cake ingredients in large bowl.

3. Combine flour, baking powder, and salt. Stir into egg mixture, mixing until smooth. Spread half of batter in greased 9" x 13" (23-cm x 33-cm) cake pan. Arrange apples over top. Sprinkle half of topping mixture over apples. Spread remaining batter over top. Sprinkle with remaining topping.

4. Bake at 350°F (180°C) for 50–60 minutes, or until cake springs back when lightly touched. Serve warm or cool.

Makes about 16 servings.

(The Easy Apple Cake is included in the photo following p. 203.)

Raisin Soda Bread

2 cups	all-purpose flour	500 ml
2 tbsp	sugar	30 ml
1 tbsp	baking powder	15 ml
½ tsp	baking soda	2 ml
½ tsp	salt	2 ml
½ cup	butter	125 ml
½ cup	raisins *(optional)*	125 ml
¾ cup	buttermilk *or* sour milk	175 ml

A quick and easy alternative when you run out of bread. Great toasted.

1. Combine first 5 ingredients in a large bowl. Cut in butter with pastry blender or 2 knives to make small crumbs. Stir in raisins.

2. Add buttermilk to flour mixture, stirring just until moistened. Dough will be crumbly. Turn out onto lightly floured surface. Knead lightly 12–15 times or until a smooth ball forms. Place on lightly greased baking sheet. Pat dough out to a circle about 7" (18 cm) in diameter. With sharp knife, score top of dough with a large X.

3. Bake at 425°F (220°C) for 20–25 minutes, or until golden. Serve warm.

Makes 1 loaf.

TIP:

To sour milk, put 1 tbsp (15 ml) lemon juice or vinegar in a measuring cup. Add milk to make ¾ cup (175 ml) or 1 cup (250 ml) as recipe requires. Let stand 5 minutes; stir well.

Overleaf, clockwise from top left: Chocolate Chip Crisps (p. 195), Mix-in-the-Pan Cake (p. 206), Easy Apple Cake (p. 202), Baking Powder Biscuits with cheese (p. 201), and Raisin Soda Bread (this page).

Mix-in-the-Pan Cake

Cake

1½ cups	all-purpose flour	375 ml
1 cup	sugar	250 ml
¼ cup	cocoa	60 ml
1 tsp	baking powder	5 ml
1 tsp	baking soda	5 ml
¼ tsp	salt	1 ml
⅓ cup	butter, *melted*	75 ml
1 tbsp	lemon juice *or* **vinegar**	15 ml
1 cup	warm water	250 ml

Frosting

1 cup	brown sugar, *packed*	250 ml
¼ cup	milk	60 ml
2 tbsp	butter	30 ml
3 tbsp	icing sugar	45 ml

A moist chocolate cake that you mix and bake all in one pan – what could be easier? There's no egg in this cake, so it's ideal for the days you forget to pack the eggs or someone eats the last few for breakfast. The brown-sugar frosting is different and delicious, but for convenience you can substitute a ready-to-serve brand or your home-made family favourite.

1. Combine first 6 dry ingredients in an ungreased 8" (20-cm) square cake pan. Mix well.

2. Add butter, lemon juice, and water. Mix well with fork until smoothly blended.

3. Bake at 350°F (180°C) for 35–40 minutes, or until cake springs back when lightly touched. Cool slightly.

4. Combine first 3 frosting ingredients in a medium saucepan. Boil 2 minutes. Cool slightly.

5. Beat in icing sugar until smooth and starting to thicken (about 5 minutes). Spread right away on warm cake. (Icing hardens quickly.)

Makes about 9 servings.

TIP:
• The cake is so moist it's also delicious without frosting, perhaps topped with a dollop of whipped cream.

(Mix-in-the-Pan Cake is included in the photo on the preceeding page.)

Blueberry Streusel Coffee Cake

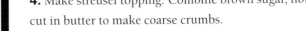

Maybe it was the company, or the beautiful morning on Lake of Bays, or the fact that this cake contains 2 whole cups of blueberries – but it stands out in my memory as a truly delicious way to begin the day.

Cake

2 cups	flour	500 ml
2 tsp	baking powder	10 ml
½ tsp	salt	2 ml
¾ cup	sugar	175 ml
¼ cup	soft butter	60 ml
1	large egg	
½ cup	milk	125 ml
	zest of 1 lemon, *grated*	
2 cups	blueberries	500 ml

Topping

½ cup	brown sugar	125 ml
⅓ cup	flour	75 ml
½ tsp	cinnamon	2 ml
¼ cup	butter	60 ml

1. Combine flour, baking powder, and salt, and set aside.

2. Cream butter with sugar until fluffy. Beat in egg and milk.

3. With quick strokes, blend liquid ingredients into flour mixture and fold in lemon zest and blueberries. Spoon batter into a greased 9" x 9" (23-cm x 23-cm) pan.

4. Make streusel topping: Combine brown sugar, flour, and cinnamon, then cut in butter to make coarse crumbs.

5. Cover cake batter with topping. Bake at 375°F (190°C) for about 45 minutes, until a toothpick inserted in the centre of the cake comes out clean.

Serves 8.

Peaches & Raspberries in Wine

1 bottle	dry Italian white wine	750 ml
½ cup	sugar	125 ml
4 strips	orange peel (¾" x 2"/2 cm x 5 cm)	
3	cinnamon sticks	
6	fresh peaches	
5 cups	fresh raspberries	1.25 L

TIP:

• Nectarines and strawberries prepared exactly the same way are another cottage favourite.

When unexpected company arrives, serve this wonderful-looking dessert over ice cream – it's delicious and stretches the fruit to serve more people.

1. Combine 1 cup (250 ml) wine, sugar, orange peel, and cinnamon sticks in a small saucepan. Cook over low heat, stirring until sugar dissolves. Increase heat to medium and simmer 15 minutes, stirring occasionally. Remove from heat. Stir in remaining wine. Cool completely.

2. Blanch peaches; remove skin (see Tips, p. 183) and slice.

3. Combine peaches, raspberries, and spiced wine in glass serving bowl. Chill at least 1 hour before serving.

Makes about 8 servings.

QUICK TRICK:

To make a quick Raspberry Sauce for ices or ice cream, dissolve ¼ cup (60 ml) sugar in ¼ cup (60 ml) water in a small pan over moderate heat. Add the juice of 1 lemon. Put the mixture in a blender or food processor with 2 cups (500 ml) of fresh or frozen raspberries and whirl until smooth. (Press through a sieve to remove seeds if you like.) Store in a covered jar in the refrigerator.

Peaches & Raspberries in Wine is an elegant, not-too-sweet dessert. The Caramel-Pecan Sticky Buns (p. 210) are at the other extreme – rich and deliciously gooey.

Caramel-Pecan Sticky Buns

2 cups	pecan halves *or* **pieces**	500 ml
1 bag	**frozen white dinner-roll dough** *(3 lbs/1.3 kg)*	
1 pkg	**butterscotch pudding and pie filling** *(not instant)* *(6 oz/170 g)*	
½ cup	**butter,** *cut in small pieces*	125 ml
½ cup	**brown sugar,** *lightly packed*	125 ml

TIPS:

• Enjoy leftover frozen rolls baked as directed on package. Or keep them frozen and save them up for another batch of sticky buns.

• Save the leftover pudding mix. When you've made 3 batches of sticky buns, you'll have enough mix for 1 more batch.

What a treat to wake up to warm rolls smothered in a caramel sauce with lots of pecans. This recipe is a cook's delight – requiring little preparation, thanks to convenience foods. The buns are prepared ahead and rise overnight, leaving only the baking when you get up in the morning.

1. Spray a 9" (3-L) bundt or tube pan with non-stick cooking spray or grease lightly with shortening. Spread pecans in bottom of pan.

2. Arrange frozen rolls closely together in single layer over pecans. (Use about 25 rolls.)

3. Measure out ¾ of pudding mix – about ⅔ cup (150 ml). Sprinkle mix evenly over rolls. Scatter butter pieces on top; sprinkle with brown sugar.

4. Cover loosely with plastic wrap or greased foil. Let stand at room temperature for 6–9 hours, or until buns are just below top of pan. Rising time will vary depending on how warm or cool your "room temperature" is.

5. Place pan on a piece of aluminum foil or a baking sheet to catch any drips that run over. Bake at 350°F (180°C) for 30–35 minutes, or until golden brown and firm, and buns sound hollow when lightly tapped.

6. Immediately after removing from oven, loosen buns from sides of pan and invert onto serving plate. Enjoy warm, cool, or reheated, if there are any left.

Makes about 8 servings.

(The Caramel-Pecan Sticky Buns are shown in the photo on the previous page.)

Almond Toffee Bars

30	graham cracker squares *(approx.)*	
1 cup	butter	250 ml
1 cup	brown sugar, *packed*	250 ml
½ cup	almonds, *sliced*	125 ml

A quick crispy sweet that's wonderful served with ice cream. No-one will guess how simple these cookies are.

1. Lay graham cracker squares in a single layer to line the bottom of a thoroughly buttered jelly-roll pan (about 10" x 15"/25 cm x 38 cm). Trim to make them fit so they form a nice flat base.

2. In a medium saucepan, melt butter over low heat. Add sugar and stir until mixture comes together, about 3–4 minutes. (Don't let it get too hot.) Stir in almonds.

3. Pour toffee mixture over graham crackers. Bake in 375°F (190°C) oven 7–8 minutes. (Do not overbake.)

4. Let cool about half an hour, then slice into small fingers.

Makes lots.

QUICK TRICKS:

Slices of fresh pineapple caramelized on the grill are a wonderful and simple dessert. Select firm, ripe pineapples. Cut away the top and bottom, remove skin and eyes, and slice into rings about ½" (1 cm) thick. Cook on the grill until the edges begin to brown and caramelize. Serve the slices hot with a sprinkle of brown sugar and a splash of rum.

• You can do bananas in a similar fashion. Slit each banana through the skin and down one side. Sprinkle a squeeze of lemon or lime juice and a spoonful of brown sugar in the slit. Cook on the grill, split side up, until just soft to the touch, about 5 minutes. Remove from fire and remove top flaps of peel. Sprinkle banana with a little more brown sugar and lemon or lime juice, and add a couple of splashes of rum. Serve hot with a spoon.

Double-Crust Mixed-Fruit Pie

Pastry

pastry for a 2-crust pie *(recipe on p. 215)*

Filling

2 cups	apples, *peeled and sliced*	500 ml
1 cup	rhubarb, *sliced*	250 ml
³⁄₄ cup	raspberries	175 ml
1 cup	sugar	250 ml
¹⁄₄–¹⁄₃ cup	all-purpose flour	60–75 ml
1	egg, *beaten*	

Topping

2 tsp	milk	10 ml
2 tsp	sugar	10 ml

A lovely combination of fresh fruits baked to perfection in a glistening, tender, golden-brown crust.

1. Combine all filling ingredients. (Use the extra flour if fruit is quite juicy.)

2. On a floured board, roll out half the pastry. Fit into a 9" (23-cm) pie plate. Fill with fruit mixture.

3. Roll out remaining pastry and place over fruit. Trim extra pastry off bottom and top crusts, leaving about ¹⁄₂" (2 cm) beyond the outer edge of pie plate. Fold top edge under bottom, seal, and flute around rim. Cut vents in top crust.

4. Brush top crust lightly with milk and sprinkle with sugar. Bake on bottom shelf of oven at 400°F (200°C) for 10 minutes, then reduce heat to 350°F (180°C) and bake 30–35 minutes longer, or until fruit is tender. Cool on wire rack.

Makes about 6 servings.

The pies have it: Double-Crust Mixed-Fruit Pie (this page) and Muskoka Blueberry Pie (p. 214).

Muskoka Blueberry Pie

¾ cup	sugar	175 ml
2½ tbsp	cornstarch	35 ml
⅔ cup	water	150 ml
4 cups	fresh wild blueberries	1 L
2 tbsp	butter	30 ml
1	**lemon,** *grated rind and juice*	
2 tbsp	orange liqueur	30 ml
1	**baked pie shell** *9"/23 cm (see Basic Pastry, facing page)*	
	whipped cream	

TIP:

• Replace blueberries with raspberries, or combine a mixture of summer berries for another great taste.

This version of the summer classic gets its wonderful flavour from a combination of cooked and raw berries and its name from the lakes region north of Toronto.

1. Combine sugar, cornstarch, water, and 1 cup (250 ml) blueberries in a small saucepan. Bring to a boil, then simmer, stirring constantly until thickened, about 10–15 minutes. (Time will vary with moisture in berries.)

2. Remove from heat and add butter, lemon rind and juice, and liqueur. Mix well. Chill at least 1 hour.

3. Remove sauce from refrigerator about 1 hour before serving. Fold in remaining berries. Spoon into pie shell. Chill 1 hour.

4. To serve, top with whipped cream, or serve each piece with a dollop of whipped cream or a scoop of vanilla or maple walnut ice cream.

Makes 6–8 servings.

(The Muskoka Blueberry Pie is shown in the photo opposite p. 213.)

Basic Pastry

2 cups	all-purpose flour	500 ml
¾ tsp	salt	4 ml
1 cup	shortening	250 ml
1	egg	
2 tbsp	ice water	30 ml
1 tbsp	white vinegar	15 ml

Use this easy-to-work pastry for both sweet and savoury pies.

1. Combine flour and salt in a mixing bowl. Cut in shortening until mixture resembles coarse crumbs.

2. Combine the egg, water, and vinegar. Pour onto the flour mixture and stir with a fork until all of the mixture is moistened.

3. Gather the dough into a ball, then divide in two. On a floured surface, flatten 1 ball into a circle and turn it over to flour both sides.

4. Roll dough to a uniform thickness, flouring the rolling pin and surface as necessary to prevent sticking.

5. Transfer dough to pie plate. Trim and flute. Fill and bake as specified in recipe. Or prick unfilled shell and bake at 425°F (220°C) for 12–15 minutes.

Makes enough pastry for a double-crust pie.

TIPS:

• Roll pastry and shape in pie plates. Stack, wrap well, and store in freezer. A pie, tart, or quiche can then be ready for the oven in minutes.

• Make roll-ups if you have leftover pastry after you've trimmed your pie crust: Roll the pastry out again and spread lightly with butter. Sprinkle with brown sugar and cinnamon, and roll up like a jelly roll, pinching ends to seal. Place on a baking sheet. (Line with foil for easy cleanup.) Bake at 350°F (180°C) for about 20 minutes until crisp. Cool slightly, then cut in slices.

Chewy Butterscotch Bars

¼ cup	butter	60 ml
1 cup	brown sugar, *packed*	250 ml
1	egg	
1½ tsp	vanilla	7 ml
¾ cup	all-purpose flour	175 ml
1 tsp	baking powder	5 ml
¼ tsp	salt	1 ml
⅔ cup	nuts, *chopped*	150 ml

This recipe takes only a few minutes to put together – and all the ingredients are mixed in one saucepan.

1. Melt butter in medium saucepan. Stir in brown sugar, egg, and vanilla. Mix well.

2. Add remaining ingredients, stirring until smooth. Spread evenly in greased 8" (20-cm) square cake pan.

3. Bake at 325°F (160°C) for 25–30 minutes. Cool, then cut into squares.

Makes about 20 bars.

QUICK TRICK:

Always have at least one lemon cake mix on hand in the cupboard. For a delicious cake to serve with berries or tropical fruits, mix up the "richer" version using extra oil and eggs, following the instructions on the box. Reduce the water required by ¼ cup (60 ml) and soak ¼ cup (60 ml) poppy seeds in ¼ cup (60 ml) milk for a few minutes. Stir mixture into the batter. Combine 1 tbsp (15 ml) each of cinnamon, cocoa, and sugar. Spoon half the batter into a greased bundt or angel food cake pan and sprinkle half the spice mixture over the batter. Spoon in the remaining batter and sprinkle with the rest of the spice mixture. Bake according to box directions.

Blueberry Bread Pudding
with Blueberry Sauce

1 loaf	day-old challah *or* other sweet eggbread *or* white French country bread, *cut in 1"(2-cm) cubes*	
3 cups	milk	750 ml
1 cup	sugar	250 ml
good pinch	cinnamon	
1 tsp	vanilla	5 ml
2 cups	fresh blueberries	500 ml
6	eggs	
	Blueberry Sauce	

Blueberry Sauce

2 cups	blueberries	500 ml
½ cup	orange juice	125 ml
1 tsp	orange zest, *grated*	5 ml
2 tbsp	sugar	30 ml
1 tsp	cornstarch *dissolved in ¼ cup (60 ml) cold water*	5 ml

TIP:

•Raisins, chopped dried apricots, or other berries can be substituted for the blueberries.

Bread pudding is an old-fashioned dessert that has come back into vogue, and this version is wonderful to make during blueberry season. Any day-old bread can form the base as long as it has good taste and texture and is not so assertive that it dominates the flavour of the eggs and berries.

1. Soak bread in milk for 1 hour. Mix in sugar, cinnamon, vanilla, and blueberries.

2. Whisk eggs and fold into mixture. Pour into a 10" (25-cm) lightly buttered springform pan, or equivalent large baking dish, and bake at 350°F (180°C) for about 1 hour or until a toothpick inserted in the centre comes out clean.

3. Cool slightly before removing from the springform pan, or serve directly from the baking dish. Serve warm, with Blueberry Sauce on top and cream or custard alongside.

Serves 6–8.

Blueberry Sauce

1. Combine all ingredients in a small, heavy saucepan. Set over medium heat and stir while sauce comes to a boil. Set aside to cool.

Makes about 2 cups (500 ml).

Index

Recipe variations have also been indexed; therefore, when looking up a recipe from a listing in the index, also check the "Tips" and "Quick Tricks" sections on the page.

Recipe variations have also been indexed; therefore, when looking up a recipe from a listing in the index, also check the "Tips" and "Quick Tricks" sections on the page.

Recipe variations have also been indexed; therefore, when looking up a recipe from a listing in the index, also check the "Tips" and "Quick Tricks" sections on the page.

Recipe variations have also been indexed; therefore, when looking up a recipe from a listing in the index, also check the "Tips" and "Quick Tricks" sections on the page.